Mother of Ten

By JB Rowley

(This book is the sequel to *Whisper My Secret*.)

Published by:
Potoroo Press 2013
P.O. Box 235
Albert Park, Victoria, Australia.

Please note: This book uses British English spelling. Readers who are used to American English might notice a difference in the spelling of some words.

Print Edition

Dedication

This book is dedicated to all mothers who have had to suffer the pain of forced separation from their children and all children who have had to grow up without knowing their mothers.

Acknowledgements

Thank you to:

Anita Marshall and Judi Hillyear for their generous editorial support with *Mother of Ten*.

Friends who helped me with research and memories.

Members of my family who helped me with my research and memories, with special thanks to my Dopper siblings, Kenny, Valerie, Allan, and their families.

The courageous Australians who told their stories for the public record: mothers who were separated from their children and people who, as children, were separated from their families and placed in out-of-home 'care'.

All those who read *Whisper My Secret* and all those who supported *Whisper My Secret* in other ways.

To the members of the Friday Writers' Group and the Writers' Lunch Group for their invaluable feedback during the writing of *Mother of Ten* and for being 'on my team'.

Preface

In this second and final part of my mother's memoir I have tried to give a fuller picture of her life and, at the request of readers, the lives of her first three children. On occasion, I have used quotes from other mothers who suffered a similar trauma to try to give you a stronger sense of what my mother might have experienced. Likewise, to supplement the stories of my half-siblings I have used quotes from other Australians who lived through similar childhoods.

Note: When I wrote *Whisper My Secret* I used real names for some people and false names for others. I have since been persuaded that pseudonyms are not necessary. However, changing the names from the pseudonyms to real names in *Mother of Ten* would create confusion for those who have read *Whisper My Secret* so I have arrived at a compromise. In most cases I have continued to use the false names used in *Whisper My Secret*. In such instances I have adopted the following strategy: when the pseudonym is first mentioned in *Mother of Ten* I have also given the real name in brackets but thereafter continued to use the pseudonym. Furthermore, real names for all those who have been given a pseudonym are included at the end of the book.

Where I have judged it would create minimal or no confusion to readers I have changed the false names used in *Whisper My Secret* to real names in *Mother of Ten*.

They are as follows:

Billy (George & Myrtle's 1st child) has been changed to his real name: **Bobby**.

Tommy (George & Myrtle's 2nd child) has been changed to his real name: **Maxie**. **Thomas Andrew Webb** (Myrtle's adoptive father) has been changed to his real name: **James Jacob Webb**.

A glossary and a bibliography are also provided at the end of the book.

Chapter 1

ONE DAY WHEN I WAS around five years old I detonated with unexpected ferocity in response to the persistent teasing and aggravation of my two older brothers. I picked up a bastard file and thrust it violently at eight-year-old Maxie. The sharp end pierced the palm of his hand and ran through to the other side. Blood spurted into the air. Maxie's wail shattered the silence of the bush.

"Mu...um! She stabbed me. She stabbed me."

That was bound to get Mum's attention – and it did. She dropped the tea towel she had been holding into the cement tub that served as a kitchen sink and rushed out onto the veranda.

Bobby had both eyes fixed on the blood streaming from his younger brother's hand.

"Mum. June killed Maxie's hand," he said, eager to be the first with the news.

Mum ran over to us. Maxie's cries increased in volume at her approach. I stood with legs apart and arms hanging by my sides. As far as I was concerned, my actions had been completely justified; my brother could cry his eyes out for all I cared.

Maxie took a few faltering steps toward Mum. "She stabbed me, Mum. She stabbed me."

He held his bleeding palm up for her inspection. Bobby reached down and picked up the bastard file, its sharp point red with blood.

"With this, Mum. She threw this at him," he said.

Mum remained calm. Though the sight of the blood no doubt filled her with panic, she had a mother's experience of children's injuries and knew they often looked worse than they actually were. Just the same, she acted swiftly to get Maxie to the doctor.

Her eyes scanned the empty green paddocks next door. Nonchalant sheep rested in the shade of large gum trees growing along the fence line. In the distance, the curved corrugated roof of the shearing shed was visible but the shed stood empty and silent. It was Saturday so there was no one there – no one to help her.

Mum was on her own with us kids because my father had been away for a few days. He and the other sleeper cutters often had to camp out in the bush in order to get the trees felled and hewn into railway sleepers. We all missed him when he was away and Mum and Dad hated being apart but there was no other choice. With each new child it had become increasingly difficult to make ends meet. Paying cheap rent to live in the caretaker's cottage attached to the sheep farm in exchange for keeping an eye on the farm cut down on expenses considerably, but it also meant living several miles from town in virtual isolation. Our closest neighbours were at a dairy just over a kilometre away.

"Bobby," said Mum. "Run down to the road. Quickly! Stop the first car you see."

Bobby did not move. His fascination with his brother's bleeding hand held him rigid.

"Run!"

The tone of Mum's voice in that single word was enough to break the spell. Bobby ran. His bare feet trampled the grass as he cut across the paddock, his long lanky legs propelling him towards the highway turned so fast they looked like cartwheels.

We lived on the corner of Duggans Road and Bonang Highway, around five kilometres north of the township of Orbost in Victoria. Duggans Road was just a dirt track and Bonang Highway was a single lane gravel road. The so-called highway continued across the state border into the Snowy Mountains in New South Wales (NSW) after meandering through old growth forest areas where Australia's last bushranger, The Snowy River Bandit, roamed before being arrested near Orbost in December 1940.

When my father was away, Mum had no vehicle and no way of contacting him. In emergencies like the one I had created this day, she simply had to manage as best she could. Hailing a passing motorist was as natural for us as lifting up a phone to dial an emergency number is in today's world.

"Mu..um," cried Maxie. His hazel eyes looked up at her imploringly. Rivulets of tears had created pink streaks of clean skin on his dirty face. "My hand hurts."

Yanking off her apron, Mum squatted in front of Maxie and gently wrapped his bleeding hand in it.

"We'll get you to the hospital. You'll be all right."

She rose and urged Maxie forward with an arm across his shoulders. With her other hand she pulled me along as well and hurriedly shepherded us down to the gate and along the dirt track. Maxie's cries had subsided but, to keep Mum's attention focused on him, he emitted plaintive distress signals as we hurried along.

When we reached the highway, Bobby was standing in the middle of the road peering into the distance, turning his head occasionally to scan the road in the opposite direction.

"Nothin's comin'," he said. He looked at his brother. "Maxie'll die, won't he, Mum?" His tone was one of excited anticipation.

"Don't be silly. He's not going to die."

Mum looked at Maxie's hand. Blood had seeped through the blue gingham apron creating an ominous large red patch.

"There's nothin' comin', Mum," said Bobby again. "Nobody's gonna come today." The hint of satisfaction in his voice revealed that he was relishing the drama this bad news would add to the situation. He stood with his hands at chest level and a thumb behind each of the braces that held up his grey shorts. His large ears, exposed by Dad's amateur hair cutting skills, made him look even younger than ten. Despite this, he exuded an air of authority as he often did when, as the eldest child, he felt the need to assume the role of head of the family in his father's absence. Mum's brow creased with worry as she listened for the sound of a vehicle.

Between Orbost and Duggans Road, the Bonang Highway was bordered on the western side with farm paddocks and on the other side with bushland. People travelling through to NSW used the road and the locals used it to get to the rubbish tip which was just a couple of kilometres past our home. At the weekends people drove, walked or rode their bicycles out to 'the tip'. If they saw Mum in our yard, they would wave to her as they passed. Mum would respond with a cheerful answering wave. Sometimes that was the closest interaction she got with anyone outside the family for weeks. In fact, seeing other people was such a novelty that we would all wave energetically at passers-by.

This particular day being a Saturday Mum must have felt sure someone would be along fairly soon on their way to the tip. The minutes ticked by but we heard only the bush and the silence of distance.

Somewhere a kookaburra cackled. "Koo koo koo ka ka ka koo koo koo."

Kookaburras were common where we lived and they often came right up to the house and sat on the verandah rail. Our cottage was set back from the road. Between the house and the highway stood the chook house on one side and the 'wood heap' on the other. Beyond that was the orchard. Well, perhaps calling it an orchard is being a little grandiose. It was just a corner of the yard where several healthy fruit trees grew. Apple, plum and apricot trees contrasted with the gum trees that surrounded the property. Behind the house was a hayshed, a tool shed and a wash house. In one corner stood the dunny, camouflaged and kept cool inside by the canopy of a huge apple tree. I had been startled out of my wits on several occasions by the sound of one of the big green apples dropping on the roof of the dunny while I was occupied inside.

Time dragged by. The sharp shriek of a cockatoo cut through the bush. We waited. Finally we heard it – the far off rumbling of a car engine.

"Somethin' comin' Mum. I can hear a car," said Bobby.

It would be some time before the vehicle arrived. Sounds travel long distances in the bush so that we could hear a car even when it was still miles away. Mum pulled Maxie closer while we waited.

"We'll have you to the hospital in no time. The doctors'll fix you up and give you a big white bandage for your hand."

"It hurts, Mum."

"I know, love, but you must be brave. When your father comes home, I'll be able to tell him how brave you've been."

"I am being brave." Maxie rearranged his face in an effort to look heroic. "It doesn't hurt that much, Mum."

After a few seconds another thought occurred to Maxie. "Will I still have the bandage on when I go back to school, Mum?"

"Perhaps."

A smile brightened Maxie's teary face as he considered the possibility of showing his school mates his fully bandaged hand. I could almost hear him. "I nearly lost my hand on the holidays, I did. My sister tried to murder me." His trauma was already evolving into an adventure he could use to impress his friends.

In the centre of the road, Bobby was waving his arms in criss-cross fashion to alert the driver of the oncoming vehicle. It was coming from the town but we knew whoever it was would turn around and take us back into the hospital; that was the country way. Bobby stayed in position until the car drew close and began to slow down, stepping to the side of the road as the grey Holden came to a halt.

Tom, the driver of the car, turned out to be someone who knew my father. In a small community it is not unusual to discover that a randomly hailed motorist is an acquaintance, a friend or even a relative.

Bobby gave Tom the news bulletin: "My sister tried to kill my brother."

Maxie thrust his bloodied, wrapped hand under Tom's nose. I remained sullen and silent; sure I had been justified on the grounds of self-defence.

"That looks like a serious war wound, young fella," said Tom. "You'd better hold your hand upright to stop the blood running away."

After helping us all into the car, Tom drove down to the house so that my mother could collect the twins who were sleeping in their shared cot. Then, with Bobby and Maxie oozing importance in the front passenger seat and the rest of us squashed into the back, we headed into town.

At the hospital, the doctor assured my mother that Maxie's injury was not as serious as it looked but needed 'a few stitches and a bandage'.

Chapter 2

WORD WAS SENT TO MY father at the timber workers' camp about what had happened to Maxie's hand. He came home as soon as he heard. Bobby and Maxie were excited about his return, jubilantly anticipating the punishment he would inflict on me.

When our old green truck rattled down Duggans Road and turned into the gate, Bobby, Maxie and I raced to greet Dad, clambering onto the back of the truck as it slowed down. Mum stood on the veranda outside the kitchen door, wiping her hands on her apron. With her head slightly to one side as was her habit and a quizzical smile hovering on her lips, she waited for the truck to pull up. Out stepped my father, tall with thick dark hair and deep brown eyes. The sleeves of his shirt were rolled up to reveal the muscles of a bushman under tanned skin. We all clamoured around him. He lifted me up over his head and bounced me on his hands while my brothers eagerly broke the news about what I had done.

"Look what June did to Maxie, Dad," said Bobby.

"She stabbed me," said Maxie, holding up his bandaged hand.

The clean white dressing the doctor had wrapped his injured hand in the day before was already a grubby grey. Maxie and Bobby were severely disappointed because on this occasion my father did not punish me. All he did was look from Maxie's hand to my mother as he placed me gently back on the ground. Later, when we were all out in the yard, I heard him talking to Mum about me.

"She's just learning to stick up for herself, love. You said yourself she rarely says boo to her brothers – just runs away and hides when they tease her. She's got four brothers now so she'll have to learn to hold her own. Might of gone a bit overboard this time but the boys musta given her good reason."

Dad had just finished chopping a pile of wood while we watched, the sun glinting on the blade as he swung the axe high over his right shoulder. His right hand slid smoothly along the wooden handle to rest next to his left hand as the axe came back down. The blade sliced the mahogany log expertly along the middle to expose its red wood. Bobby and Maxie stood side by side as they observed their father. Balancing two-year-old Georgie on her left hip, my mother stood close enough to the woodheap to stop the older boys should either of them show any sign of moving too close to where Dad was working with the axe. I stood next to my mother with one arm clutching Kevin tightly around the middle to restrain him.

We had watched as the mahogany pieces fell from the chopping block and lay in the sawdust next to the pile of ironbark my father had previously cut. Then he swung the axe one last time and brought it down hard so that it was embedded in the chopping block. He pulled a much-used handkerchief from his overalls pocket, wiped the sweat from his brow and glanced across at Mum, grinning. With a playful look in his eye he returned the handkerchief to its pocket and gripped her around the waist with both hands. She threw her head back and laughed.

"Put me down, Dad."

"I won't drop you, Mum. You're as light as a feather."

He held her close. Their eyes locked for a second before she laughed again and released herself from his grasp, her face flushed.

"Not in front of the children, Dad," she said as she smoothed her apron. "I thought you wanted a smoke, anyway."

He smiled, eyeing her with admiration, and leaned his tall, muscular body up against the water tank.

"You know who you remind me of?"

Mum shook her head.

"Greer Garson. That's who. You're the spitting image."

"Stop your nonsense, Dad," she said.

She laughed off the compliment but I could tell she was pleased. With her long hair curling away from her face and rolled up at the back, she did look a little like a 1940s film actress.

I watched and observed; a silent five-year-old. I loved to study my father, taking note of his every movement as though he were a work of art. I guess it's a thing girls do at a certain stage of their lives.

He reached into the pocket of his khaki shirt for his packet of tobacco and took out a slip of cigarette paper before returning the packet to his pocket. Holding the strip of white paper in one hand he dipped his free hand into the tobacco, pinched out a clump, placed it on the paper, and spread it along the middle before deftly rolling the tobacco into a cylindrical shape. He then rolled the paper around the tobacco, licking along each edge and pressing the edges together to form a rough cigarette. Reaching into his pocket for his matches he placed the cigarette between his lips then struck a match against the side of the match box. He held the flame to the tip of his hand-made cigarette until the end burned red. Shaking the match to ensure it was completely extinguished, he threw it to the ground and returned the box of matches to his shirt pocket. This procedure was always done in a state of silent concentration so Mum waited. When he had finished, she resumed the conversation about me.

"Yes, she did go overboard and it could have been a lot worse. She needs to learn restraint. She can't let her temper get the better of her like that."

My father drew on his cigarette and exhaled a cloud of smoke into the air.

"Don't worry, Mum. It's not likely to happen again. I bet Maxie'll be treating her with more caution from now on, and young Bobby too."

He grinned at me and winked. "Eh, Brigid?" he said.

Brigid was his pet name for me. I don't remember him ever calling me June. I thought that Brigid was a name all fathers called their daughters. Funny, the ideas we get in our heads as kids!

I hoped he was right about Maxie and Bobby. Having so many brothers was not exactly a dream come true for me. I had discovered they could be challenging to say the least although my brothers were no different to most young country boys of the day. Living out on the Bonang Highway we were isolated by poverty, lack of public transport and lack of communication technology. Having little social interaction with other families meant I had no girls on which to model myself. Instead, I fought fiercely to be one of the boys.

However, to Bobby and Maxie I was just an annoying little girl they did not deign to take seriously. They often indulged in the apparently hilarious sport of teasing me; their primary goal being to provoke a reaction. Often my response was to run away in tears and hide in the hayshed where I always had a book hidden somewhere in the musty bales. By the time I finished the book and emerged from the hayshed my brothers' deeds were long forgotten. This was not entirely satisfactory to Bobby and Maxie so they continually sought strategies that might provoke a more entertaining reaction. Sometimes they would achieve gratification when I exploded in a furious rage and cried and screamed and threw things at them. They would laugh uproariously and dodge the stones or sticks that came their way and, satisfied that their sport had resulted in the desired outcome, would wander off supremely triumphant.

The long summer holidays when there was no school created conditions ripe for sibling tensions to simmer. They had simmered to boiling point the day I 'killed Maxie's hand'.

Looking back, I think my mother must have despaired of ever moulding me into a 'typical' girl. I was a bush urchin with hard-soled feet from running around without shoes who loved climbing trees and chasing lizards.

Like the creatures of the bush, I could make myself almost invisible and was often an unnoticed silent observer listening to my parents' conversations.

"I don't like you being here on your own when I'm away," said my father one evening as he and my mother prepared to share a pot of tea. He removed his worn navy beret, once part of his Australian army uniform, and ran his fingers through his thick black hair disturbing curled shreds of sawdust. Tossing the beret up onto a coat hook, he grinned when it landed on its target. As he sat down, he lifted the enamel mug Mum had just filled with hot tea.

"I'm all right," said my mother. She drank her tea from a floral china tea cup, which had a chip on the rim. My father's enamel mug was much more practical but Mum liked to drink from pretty china cups, even chipped ones.

"It's not as if I'm completely on my own. The kids are here."

"That's what I'm thinking about," said Dad. "There's always some sort of emergency with kids.

You have no way of getting into town in a hurry if you don't have a car here."

"Stop worrying, Dad."

Husbands and wives often called each other Mum and Dad in front of their children in those days. I assume it was to ensure the children did not develop the 'disrespectful' habit of calling their parents by their given names. It became a habit so that they often forgot to use other forms of address even when the kids were not present or perhaps in large families there was always a risk of children overhearing their conversations.

"It would help if we had the telephone on," continued my father.

"And how are we going to afford that?"

Dad leant back, moving his shoulder blades against the wooden back of the chair to scratch his back.

"I could speak to Mum and Dad. They might be able to lend me some money. They'll help if they can."

Mum released a deep sigh. "You already owe them money. It'll just prey on your mind if you owe them more."

"I know. But...well, it preys on my mind leaving you and the kids here when I am out at the camp."

"Well, women have managed on their own in the

middle of nowhere in this country for years. If they can do it, I can do it."

Her words were brave, but her tone held an underlying sense of helplessness. Dad reached across the table and touched Mum's hand.

"You know I wouldn't leave you here on your own if I could help it."

"I know."

Chapter 3

AS A CHILD, IT NEVER occurred to me that my mother, the woman who so efficiently handled our childhood emergencies, the woman who was a constant nurturing presence in our lives, carried a painful secret buried deep within her. I first came upon her hidden anguish when I was three years old.

The day had turned cool. Mum slipped a cardigan over my shoulders. She helped me put my arms in the sleeves and was about to finish off the process with an embrace when I pushed her away, flinging a defiant look at her. How dare she treat me like a baby? My wrath melted, however, when our eyes met briefly for I was looking into two deep wells of pain.

Mum quickly recovered herself and applied a smile to her face. As the years passed I saw that smile again from time to time. It was not her usual smile which spread easily across her face, radiating to her eyes to linger there like sunlight dancing on an emerald ocean. This smile was a facsimile, a brave attempt at the original that lacked its joie de vivre.

That I have never forgotten this incident is indicative of the impact it had on me although as a kid I did not know why it was significant. I think my child's instinct told me my mother's reaction was not only out of proportion to the event but also out of character. Mum was not an emotional person and had a reserve that, apart from the usual mother's anger at naughty children, was usually unruffled only by laughter.

After that day, my mother never tried to hug me again. It wasn't until I discovered her secret that I realised why my rejection of her during a normal childhood developmental stage of independence had caused the anguish that was submerged in the depths of her being to charge to the surface.

Before I continue, in chapter five, the story of our lives out on the Bonang Highway, further background information is necessary.

In *Whisper My Secret* I wrote about my mother's heartbreaking forced separation from her first three children; all under the age of five. Growing up in a family of seven kids I always thought of Mum as the mother of seven when in actual fact she was the mother of ten.

As revealed in *Whisper My Secret*, my mother

Myrtle Webb became pregnant in 1938, at the age of eighteen, to Henry Bishop (Keith Dopper). He was an older boy who lived in the house next door to the flat where Myrtle and her widowed mother lived. Henry and Myrtle married in haste. They had three children between 1939 and 1941: Bertie (Kenny), Audrey (Valerie) and Noel (Allan). However, their marriage was not a happy one.

By this time Australia had become involved in World War Two and Henry Bishop was one of the many young men deployed overseas with the AIF (Australian Imperial Forces). Henry's mother, Agnes (Eva), who did not approve of her daughter-in-law, made up her mind that Myrtle was an unfaithful wife. This woman's imagination sparked unkind and spiteful gossip. Agnes and Henry eventually used Myrtle's sullied reputation to have the marriage dissolved. Henry obtained legal custody of their three children but placed them in care. Myrtle was not to be reunited with them. It was during this turmoil that Myrtle and George met.

Despite the tragedy of losing her three children, the trauma of her marriage breakdown and the shame of an unjustly tarnished reputation, Myrtle started a new life and a new family with George in Orbost. Apart from those two, no one else in our family and no one else in Orbost knew about Myrtle's previous life.

Although Myrtle was a significant distance geographically from her first three children, I am confident her emotional attachment was strong. Having no knowledge of what it was like in the orphanages, she probably took comfort from believing her children were being well looked after. This was a time when it was generally believed that children could be 'better off' in a Home. Placing kids in a Home was often seen as an appropriate course of action when times were difficult for families or even simply because both parents had to go out to work.

Myrtle was powerless to change what happened but appears to have done all that she could to maintain contact with her children and let them know she still cared about them. The overwhelming powerlessness to change a situation that robbed her of her right to be a mother to her kids must have deepened her grief at being separated from them.

Other mothers who have suffered similar experiences and professionals who work with them would not find it surprising that Myrtle kept this traumatic event secret. However, that was something that took me a long time and a lot of research to appreciate. When I learned that people suffering shock and unbearable loss develop a survival mechanism called 'a false self', I began to understand. This false self is disassociated from the self that experienced the trauma thus enabling the person to remain sane and continue their life. I can see how my mother must have done that, or something very close to it.

The traumatic impact that separation from their children has on mothers has been explored through several recent government Inquiries in Australia and other countries. In the words of Jacki, a mother whose child was taken from her at birth: 'I thank God that I was one of the stronger mothers who survived the ordeal to go on and have a relatively 'normal' life, devoid of any mental problems, drug taking, drinking, prostitution or suicide attempts. I have, instead, been married for 31 years and was fortunate enough to give birth again...' (*Releasing the Past: Mothers' stories of their stolen babies*)

Like Jacki, Myrtle managed to continue living a 'normal' life without succumbing to drugs, alcohol, depression or any of the other tragic consequences often suffered. I believe that the survival strategy of creating a false self, as well as the love and support she received from my father, enabled her to do so.

Ironically, my mother was herself a child whose parents were forced to give her up. This was another secret that my siblings and I knew nothing about until after her death when we found, amongst her papers, the private adoption agreement between her biological parents and her adoptive parents.

Mum was born Millicent Myrtle Mills on January 18, 1920 in Culcairn in the Riverina region of NSW. Established in 1880, Culcairn was not a large town but was an important service centre for smaller towns in the area, such as Walla Walla where Myrtle's parents were living at the time of her birth.

Myrtle's biological father, Alick Harold Mills, was a twenty-six year old bricklayer originally from Melbourne, Victoria. He married nineteen-year-old Vera Myrtle Allison Johnson from Rutherglen, Victoria in 1919. I am not sure why they moved to the Riverina. Alick Mills may have been attracted by work opportunities as the region had prospered in the late 19th and early 20th centuries due to the success of its wool and agricultural industries after pastoral settlement by Europeans in the 1830s.

However, the hope of work and prosperity was evidently not fulfilled because less than six months after Millicent Myrtle's birth in January 1920, Vera and Alick were forced to give up their daughter as they were, according to the adoption agreement, 'unable to support the [said] infant'.

I don't know how this situation arose but I assume Alick was unable to get enough work to support his family. Whatever the reason, a legal agreement was entered into with a couple in Lavington, near Albury, NSW: James Jacob Webb and his wife Etti (Antonia Maria). Albury, then a country town, is now a major regional city situated 160 kilometres from the source of the Murray River near Mount Kosciuszko; an area that was once part of the Wiradjuri nation.

The love Alick and Vera had for their daughter is reflected in two of the conditions of the agreement that stated they were to be given access to her 'at all reasonable times hereafter', and if the adopting parents were to die while Millicent Myrtle was still a child, Alick and Vera were entitled to custody of her.

So, at the age of four and a half months my mother became Myrtle Webb, the daughter of James and Etti Webb. James Webb was a devoted husband and father who owned a fruit and vegetable orchard. He was twenty-four when he married Etti, five years his junior, in 1905. When they adopted Myrtle, they had been married for fifteen years with no children of their own.

Myrtle's life as the daughter of James and Etti Webb was, as far as I can find out, a contented one. She attended Lavington Public School and seems to have had a happy childhood and been brought up in a nurturing environment. She developed close relationships with her cousins Henrietta and Lily (Rose), two of the five children of Anne and Reginald

Sutherland; Etti's sister and brother-in-law.

When I met Lily on my quest to discover what happened to cause Myrtle to be separated from her first children, she told me how the three girls would often meet when their parents went into the township of Albury for shopping. Later, as teenagers and young women they attended the local Saturday night dances together. On these occasions Myrtle would stay over at the Sutherlands. The girls would whisper to each other long into the night, recalling the evening's shared fun. These dances must have been family affairs because the girls started attending when Lily was in her early teens. Although Myrtle was older then her two cousins, there was only a few years difference in their ages so all three girls would have been considered too young to go out without a chaperone. The gowns Myrtle wore to these dances were later confiscated by me as a kid. It must have pained her to see those marvellous taffeta and satin creations, probably made by her mother, reduced to a child's 'dress-ups' but she shared them with me willingly.

Perhaps it was at one of the local dances that my father, George Rowley, first met Lily after he arrived in Albury with the Australian Army. George was twenty years old in March 1941 when he left his hometown of Orbost to enlist. Thousands of army and other services personnel were sent to Albury which straddles the border of Victoria and NSW. About eighteen kilometres from Albury at Bonegilla on the Victorian side was one of Australia's largest military camps.

As far as I can work out from the hand written records of the Australian Army, George arrived in Bonegilla around August 1941. He was not a man who liked to dance so I imagine he stood awkwardly on the sidelines in the dance hall watching the lovely young women and their partners swirl around the floor. Lily told me George 'set his cap' at her but she was too young to be 'serious about men'. Myrtle would not have been attending the dances at this stage, certainly not regularly, as she was already a young mother of two, with a third child on the way. However, when George later met Myrtle his heart was lost and he never wavered in his love for her.

Chapter 4

WHEN MYRTLE ARRIVED IN ORBOST in 1944 pregnant with George's first child, she was now almost 400 kilometres from Albury where she had been forced to leave her three young children from her first marriage. At this time, her home in Orbost was with George's parents but, thankfully, her new mother-in-law welcomed her with kindness and generosity. George was still a soldier in the AIF but was desperate to be discharged so that he could go home. His desire to find a way out of the army increased after Myrtle gave birth. His letters to her reveal his distress at being separated from his wife and child.

In a letter dated February 20, 1945 from Seymour, Victoria he talks of ways of getting out of the army to be with Myrtle and 'young Bobby'. If all else fails, he suggests that Myrtle and Bobby might be able to join him.

It wouldn't be much for you, love, but everybody else is getting their wife up here, I don't see why I can't be doing the same. I mean I seem to be the loneliest guy about here, Myrtle.

He returns to the idea later in the same letter.

I'll have to try to persuade you to come up here, love, because I can't live without you, darl. See what you've done to me, love, made me love you like that. I never think of going out with another girl. It just doesn't appeal to me anymore, darl. Yet one time I used to be the biggest flirt going … all I want in this world is to get home to you and get with you. I'm not worried about home, love, it's you I want.

On the last page of the letter he returns again, but with less optimism, to the suggestion that Myrtle and Bobby join him in Seymour.

I guess it's not much of an idea, love, because we are not in a position to afford it, are we darl?

In another letter, undated but written around the same time, he once again laments that he is unable to get out to be with her and asks if there is anything she wants.

I want you to have anything you desire, love, and if I can get it you will have it love.

Myrtle apparently asked him to get her a camera because in another letter he apologises that he was not able to get one in Seymour and promises to try to get her one in Melbourne when he is transferred to the hospital there.

Not all his letters have survived the years but they must have written daily to each other because later in the same letter he comments:

> *I haven't had a letter from you today, Myrtle. I guess I will get it this afternoon, love.*

All of his letters start with 'Dearest Myrtle' and end with 'your ever loving husband' and several rows of kisses. Wherever he could find space on the lettergram he added more kisses and messages like 'all my love to you, darl'. He asks about his son in each letter. In one he writes:

> *Gosh, Bobby is getting a big fellow, isn't he? He's not very tall though.*

Myrtle apparently took a photo of Bobby, probably with a camera borrowed from her new mother-in-law, and sent it to George. I am not sure how tall he expected a child of less than six months to be!

Myrtle must have also made mention of Bobby being ill, for George goes on to say:

Myrtle what's this about him dying? He's not looking that bad is he love? He's not going to die – look who his parents are! Anyway, if he is sick, send me a telegram and I will see if they will give me some compassionate leave.

The reference to Myrtle's fear that Bobby might be dying is interesting. Mothers who have been separated from their babies have reported experiencing such fears with subsequent children, believing their child might die as punishment for 'abandoning' their previous child or children.

After receiving a bone graft at Heidelberg Hospital in Melbourne to repair a wrist injury, George was finally reunited with his family when he was discharged from the army in March 1945 and returned to Orbost.

The township of Orbost is a small community in the East Gippsland Shire 375 kilometres east of Melbourne. It is part of the territorial home of the Kurnai people who once occupied the whole of East Gippsland. The town is situated on the banks of the Snowy River with its mouth a picturesque ten-minute drive away.

Established in 1842, Orbost was initially a farming community but a significant timber industry developed due to the area's rich forestry resources and the 1939 fires, one of Australia's worst natural disasters. It had been a hot, dry summer during 1938 and 1939 with fires breaking out over the state. On January 13, 1939 (known as Black Friday) temperatures reached over 45 degrees Celsius. A northerly wind hit the state and the fires became one massive fire front. Seventy one people died. More than 20 000 square kilometres of land were burnt including several towns, 1300 homes and 69 sawmills.

Prior to 1939, Victoria's major sawmilling industry had been concentrated in the mountain ash forests of the Central Highlands close to Melbourne. However, the fires destroyed the bulk of the forests and mills in this area. The demand for timber to service the post-war housing boom was urgent. The sawmilling industry had to be restructured and relocated. East Gippsland, with its rich timber resources, was the ideal choice. It was the timber industry that later provided my father with an income that enabled him to (just) support his growing family.

When Myrtle and George, my mother and father, began their life together in Orbost, Australian society was similar to that in countries like the USA and Britain at the time. Mainstream Australia was predominately 'white' people descended from the early convicts and settlers who, in the main, were from the United Kingdom. England was considered 'The

Mother Country'.

People were conservative and resistant to change. New ideas, even concepts as simple and innocent as coffee espresso machines, outdoor dining and kerbside cafes were met with horrified opposition and legal wrangles. The resistance to any modification of the clearly defined roles of men and women was such that changes were inconceivable. Men were expected to fill the role of family bread winner. Women were expected to be good wives and mothers by staying at home and caring for their children and their husbands. Divorce was condemned as shameful. The woman, whose job it was to keep the family together, was considered to be at fault in the event of a marriage breakdown. There were no support services for divorcees with or without children. Any woman on her own whether a divorcee or a widow was viewed with suspicion. They were often socially excluded, especially in country towns.

Australian society was transformed during the 1950s by thousands of new migrants from Britain, Greece, Italy and other European countries. These were boom times for the island continent. The national shortage of workers was filled by the new migrants who were employed on construction projects such as the Snowy Mountains Hydro-Electric Scheme, which diverted water from the Snowy River to make electricity.

With a growing family and little money, my parents would not have had time to think too much about the changes taking place in Australia. By this time, Orbost was well established as a prosperous centre for forestry and agricultural industries and a service town for the outlying areas with a population of approximately 2000. In the 1950s, Orbost's local timber industry began to expand dramatically in response to Australia's need for timber to supply the building trade. Dad, who trained as a butcher's apprentice before the war and worked on local farms immediately after the war, had now joined the timber industry where future prospects were promising.

Chapter 5

SOMETIMES, DURING THE SCHOOL HOLIDAYS and at weekends, Dad would take us all out to the woodcutters' camp.

There were men everywhere, some with axes and some with saws: strong men with the broad shoulders and calloused hands of hard-working bushmen. White Australians with faces tanned to mahogany brown from daily exposure to the sun were barely discernible from Aboriginal Australians. Some men worked with shirt sleeves rolled up, revealing their tanned forearms. Others wore blue or white singlets fully exposing their muscled arms. They all wore long pants and boots and most heads were covered by hats or berets.

The work environment of these tough men exposed them to danger at every turn. Death could claim any one of them without notice. Men were sometimes killed when trapped under trees or tractors or killed in accidents with machinery. If they were bitten by a spider or a snake they had to do the best they could without medical expertise. Accidents with a saw or axe could result in injuries; serious and not so serious. Men with finger tips missing, half a finger or a toe missing were not an unusual sight among the timber workers.

They worked ten to twelve hours a day for six days of the week with Sundays reserved for sharpening tools and any housekeeping they deemed necessary to do. What time they had free was spent playing cards, telling tales and singing songs.

Despite the rough conditions, they were a happy lot; calling through the trees to each other, insulting each other with cheerful grins and joking together. Italians, Australians and men from Eastern Europe worked and lived as a large family unit. Most of them were family men who enjoyed having Mum and us kids visit. When we arrived, they waved to us and called out various welcomes.

"G'day." "Ciao." "Hey, kids."

Working out in the bush and camping out for a week or more at a time, the men became accustomed to using uninhibited language so one of them would issue a warning for everyone to be careful when we were there.

"Righto, you blokes, mind your Ps and Qs now."

Mum smiled in acknowledgement of their respect.

My brothers and I loved to watch the felling of a tree. When we saw Dad sizing up a tall tree we could hardly contain our excitement.

"Are you going to chop down a tree?" my brothers asked.

"Maybe," said my father, revealing his broad forehead as he pushed his hat back slightly and craned his neck to scan the line of the tree.

He was assessing the distance and direction of the tree's drop to make sure it would fall clear of other trees. Plummeting branches from above, or 'widow makers' as the men called them, were swift and silent killers. Affected branches that did not break off were even worse because, although they stayed on the tree, they could fall at anytime, catching workers below unawares to cause serious injury or death. Dad also needed to make sure everyone was clear of the path the tree would fall along.

The other men continued with their work: some trimmed fallen trees and cut away any remaining branches, some men barked trimmed trees and pairs of men with crosscut saws sliced trunks into logs. Dad, sleeves already rolled up, took up his axe and stood legs apart by the tree. Mum gathered us into a spot where we would be safe but still able to observe.

We watched Dad's lithe body and supple movements, as he brought his axe down swiftly stroke after stroke, to cut a scarf in the tree which would guide its fall. The smell of the tree's sap was stronger with each blow.

When he was satisfied with the scarf cut, Dad went around to the other side of the tree, removing his shirt and throwing it over a tree stump as he did so. His white armless singlet revealed his broad shoulders. Wedges of wood whistled through the air as his axe cut deeper into the tree's trunk. His face showed intense concentration and perspiration oozed over his forehead and cheeks. By the time the tree began to lean forward, the damp of perspiration showed through his singlet at his shoulder blades and across his chest. He stepped clear of the tree with a glance at us to make sure we were safe.

"Timber!" he yelled.

"Timber!" My brothers exchanged grins as they echoed the call.

Everyone stopped to watch as the tree leaned and groaned. Its roots separated from earth with a creak. The lofty giant headed inexorably to the ground, shuddering through the foliage of its neighbours to land with a loud crack.

Bobby and Maxie ran to the fallen tree. They scrambled along the trunk, checking the branches for birds' nests that might have eggs in it. My mother did not usually allow them to take eggs from nests but she knew birds could not return to the nests in felled trees. Unable to find a nest, Bobby and Maxie turned their attention to the tree itself.

"Can we help with the tree, Dad?

"Yeah, can we help, Dad?"

"You can but not right now. You can help bark the tree later, if you like."

That was the job my brothers liked best: stripping the bark off the tree to unveil the smooth cream trunk, greasy with eucalyptus oil. They also loved gathering witchetty grubs which they found in some logs after the men split them. They would give them to Bluey, the camp cook, who grilled them on the coals of the fire. Witchetty grubs are the fat, wriggling white larvae of moths. I left the eating of these delicacies, much prized by the Aboriginal people, to my brothers.

Mum usually took us for a walk through the bush while Dad was working. Sometimes the bush was pretty with yellow wattles, brown boronia flowers, crimson bottlebrush or gum trees with bluish leaves. The smell of tree bark and eucalyptus oil fused with the smell of earth and damp leaves on the ground. When you are deep in the bush it is not hard to understand why the Aboriginal people believe *mrarts* (ghosts of ancestors) wander there. The bush can be full of sounds one minute, birds whistling and chattering, breezes whispering and trees swishing, then deeply silent the next, creating the sense of an unseen presence. Luckily for us, *mrarts* were mostly only seen at night.

On our walks, my brothers would scramble on ahead, jumping over fallen logs, searching for animal burrows and kicking aside sticks to disturb lizards and goannas which were always too fast for them to catch. Like my brothers, I loved to run along the creek beds, stopping to catch frogs and watch them jump from my hands back into the water.

We would see beautiful birds like rainbow lorikeets and honey eaters and occasionally hear the threatening scream of the sugar glider protecting its food, perhaps from a stealthy bird. Mum would point out the wildflowers to me: native bluebells and orchids and even native buttercups. Our walk in the bush was a wilderness adventure.

The faint smell of wood smoke greeted us when we returned to the woodcutters' camp. The men had stirred the camp fire, ready for 'smoko'. That was when they stopped work and gathered around the fire, sitting on tree stumps and logs ready for tea, cake and smokes. Some of them rolled their own cigarettes and others smoked pipes. I loved the smell of pipe tobacco.

For making tea, they had an old blackened billy-can, fashioned from a tin that once contained canned peaches. A wire handle had been looped through holes punched on either side of the can. The serrated edge caused by opening the tin with a can-opener had been filed to a smooth finish. The billy was suspended over the fire on thick wire which was held up by two sticks on either side of the fire; far enough away not to catch alight. The sturdy sticks had been forked at the top to allow the wire to slip through and be held in place.

When the water in the billy was boiling, Bluey threw a handful of tea in. Bluey was a big man with thick red hair and freckles all over his face. His old hat was held together in places with large safety pins.

"Hey, Bluey," called one of the men. "That's not dynamite you're throwin' in that billy, is it?"

Bluey joined in the laughter with the men. Throwing dynamite in the billy was a standing joke. Apparently, back in the 1800s a man 'up around Buchan' took it into his head to thaw some dynamite in a billy-can over his camp fire. He thawed the dynamite but, alas, the explosion killed him instantly.

Bobby and Maxie might have been excited about the possibility of dynamite in Bluey's billy but I was glad it contained tea leaves.

After a few seconds Bluey removed the billy from the fire and placed it next to the hot coals, beating the outside of it with a stick to make the tea leaves sink to the bottom. Bobby and Maxie groaned in disappointment.

"Ooooh, isn't he going to swing the billy, Dad?"

Using centrifugal force by swinging the billy was another way of getting the tea leaves to sink to the bottom. Dad often did it when he boiled the billy at home. We all loved to watch. My brothers studied the process carefully because Dad had promised they could do it when they were old enough.

"Why don't you ask him?" Dad said.

Bobby called to Bluey. "Are ya gonna swing the billy, Bluey?"

"Handle's too hot, young fella. I'd burn me hand off," said Bluey, with a wink at my father.

"Oooooh," Bobby and Maxie chorused their disappointment.

However, Bluey moved the billy away from the coals. After a couple of minutes he checked the heat of the handle by lifting it up with a stick and gingerly tapping it with his fingers.

Bobby and Maxie waited. They nudged each other in excitement when Bluey lifted the billy from the ground. Then, with arm at full stretch, he swung the billy several times in a wide vertical circle. My brothers mimicked his swing with their own arms.

When 'the show' was over, Bluey used an old piece of cloth to protect his hands as he tilted the billy and poured strong tea into each man's enamel mug. Most of the men drank their tea black with lots of sugar; it was difficult to keep milk fresh in the bush. However, sometimes they had a can of Sunshine Full Cream Powdered Milk and could throw some into their mugs of tea or mix the powder with water to make liquid milk. My mother often made milk the same way at home.

Mum usually baked a couple of Madeira cakes for the men for their morning tea. She cut off a large slice for each worker. They tucked into her cakes and devoured them in seconds. Except for the occasional appreciative grunt when eating Mum's cake, most of the men were quiet during smoko. Bushmen were often quiet by nature but they also needed to conserve their energy for the rest of the day's work. Sometimes, however, they told us stories.

One day when we were sitting around the camp fire we heard the sound of someone not far away, chopping down a tree with an axe.

"Listen," said Bluey.

Bluey looked across at Dad and smiled.

"Matilda," said Dad.

I pricked my ears up. Matilda? I had not heard of

a woman chopping down trees.

"Can you hear her, Brigid?" said my father.

I nodded. I was about to ask who Matilda was but Dad continued.

"That's Matilda," he said. "She copies all the sounds we make."

I still did not understand. Did that mean she wasn't really chopping down a tree? Bobby, being the eldest, already knew about Matilda so he enlightened me.

"Matilda is a lyrebird," he said.

Now I understood. I knew about lyrebirds. My mother had told me that a lyrebird was a brown bird about the size of a chook with a tail like a peacock only not as colourful. She said lyrebirds could mimic any sound they heard. However, I had not realised that they could represent the sound so accurately. Matilda's axe chopping was exactly like the real thing. Bluey grinned at my look of astonishment.

"It's Matilda all right," he said, his broad grin making his freckles dance. "She can copy anything and get it spot on like the original. And ya know what? Matilda can play the mouth organ better than me."

In the evenings it was the habit of the men to have a sing-a-long before they went to bed. Bluey played the mouth organ, some of the others played the gum leaves, someone else played a tune on a comb and somebody banged on a 44 gallon drum with a couple of sticks.

Bluey called out to the other men. "Remember that night Matilda was playin' the mouth organ?"

Voices called back. Heads nodded. Men laughed.

"She really had me goin' that night," said Bluey. "We were all just sittin' around here tired and quiet and waitin' for the billy to boil when we heard someone in the bush playin' *Waltzing Matilda* on a mouth organ. Fair dinkum! You coulda knocked me down with a feather."

"Too right!" someone called.

Bluey shook his head and laughed at the memory.

"I thought it was some codger out there in the bush," he said to me, "so we went off to see who it was but whenever we got close to the sound it'd stop. Then it'd start up again in another direction and further way. So off we'd go in the direction of the music and, blow me down, if it didn't move to another spot again, still playin' the same tune. I couldn't work it out."

"Yeah, old Bluey thought we had a ghost in the bush," someone called out. Someone else started to sing a line from the song.

And his ghost may be heard, as you camp by the billabong.

The others joined in for the last line.

You'll come a waltzing Matilda with me.

"Scared the daylights out of Bluey, did Matilda."

"He was all for packin' up camp and goin' back to town."

"Too right, I was," said Bluey. "I wasn't sleepin' out here with some ghost roamin' around in the bush."

Everyone laughed. Bluey grinned across at me and winked.

"How did you know it was Matilda?" I asked.

"Well," said Bluey, taking a long gulp of his tea. "She started singing other sounds, like the wood chopping we just heard and other birds' songs. When she mixed those up with *Waltzing Matilda*, we figured out it was a lyrebird. That's when we gave her the name Matilda. See?"

I nodded.

These days, many people believe that if you hear a lyrebird expertly mimicking sounds it must be a male. However, it was documented as early as 1908 that the female lyrebird is also an excellent mimic. On 5 October, 1908 the Adelaide newspaper *The Register* reported that 'Mr A. E. Kitson, a thoroughly competent observer and one who has a unique experience of the birds... put on record the fact that the female also is a great mimic'. The newspaper went on to list the 'curious assortment' of sounds one female lyrebird had produced in the presence of Mr Kitson.

It was one of my childhood dreams to see a lyrebird in the bush but, although we managed to find the mounds of lyrebirds I never managed to actually see one.

Lyrebirds and other bush creatures featured strongly in our lives out on the Bonang. For us, the days opened and closed with the sounds from the bush. When the morning light dawned, our rooster competed with the calls of currawongs, bellbirds, kookaburras and magpies.

In the evenings, the night air brought us the rumbling growl of possums, the chattering of nocturnal insects, frogs calling across the dam and night owls hooting 'mo…poke' through the trees. Our natural amphitheatre was vast and yet the crisp, clear sounds wrapped us in a sweet intimacy. Sometimes as I lay in my bed listening I would pick out a particular sound and smile, sure it was Matilda the mimic.

Chapter 6

THE YEAR 1956 IN AUSTRALIA saw Liberal Prime Minister Bob Menzies secure in his fourth term of government and the country in the grip of Olympic Games mania.

The Olympics were to be held in the city of Melbourne; the first time in the southern hemisphere. In fact, it was a year of firsts: the first time Australia had hosted such a large event, the first time the Olympic Games included a closing ceremony and the first time Australia's Postmaster General had issued full-colour stamps. Another significant first that year was the introduction of Australia's national television service.

However, it would be a very long time before my parents would be able to afford a television set. Their new family was expanding at a rapid rate. My mother was expecting another child to add to their brood of five: Bobby, Maxie, me and the twins, Georgie and Kevin. There was no money for luxuries such as

birthday presents. Birthdays were not even mentioned in our house probably because it was easier to
forget about them altogether than to struggle with
the problem of finding the money to buy presents.
What money Mum and Dad could put aside went
towards trying to buy Christmas presents. Mum also
saved the labels on the packets of Lan Choo tea and
redeemed them for various items. Our grandparents
bought us simple Christmas gifts and sometimes the
local shopkeepers donated goods. I remember Mr
Orme Andrews, who owned a toy shop in Orbost,
arriving at our place one Christmas with a bag of
toys for my brothers and me. My gift was a large
doll: the largest doll I had ever seen.

Feeding a growing family must have been a gru-
elling challenge for Mum. However, like most
mothers of her time, she was resourceful and constantly found new ways to make a little go a long
way. Potatoes were cheap because we grew our own.
They were excellent for filling our tummies, especially when mashed with a little butter and milk added
to make them fluffy. A mound of mashed potatoes
made our plates look overflowing with food.

Meat was expensive to buy but considered important at every meal. Sometimes we got sheep from
the farm which my father, with his butcher training,
was able to cut up expertly. Rabbit stew was often on

the menu. Rabbits were plentiful; in fact they were a pest in Australia at the time. All Dad had to do was go out and shoot them and skin them. When Mum did buy meat from the butcher, it was always the cheapest cuts. She would make minced meat 'go further' by mixing it up in a bowl with a beaten egg, breadcrumbs made from stale bread and chopped onions. This mixture was flattened out, cut into squares and fried. We all loved Mum's minced meat rissoles.

We also loved her patty cakes. These were little cakes baked in corrugated paper cups. She would bake at least one enormous tray full of those little cakes in the capacious oven of the old wood stove almost every day. When they were cooked she would protect her hands with a thick tea-towel and remove the heavy iron tray laden with hot cakes, releasing the tempting aroma to waft through the house. Like eager little mice ever on the alert for a new source of food, my brothers and I would materialise in the kitchen. Surreptitiously, our hands reached out. By the time Mum had placed the tray on the table, gaps had appeared in the evenly arranged rows of cakes but she never gave any indication that she noticed. Before too long, there was going to be another pair of hands to steal her cakes away.

I knew that when this new baby arrived, Mum

would have her Box Brownie camera out. As soon as possible after the birth of a new child, she took a family shot. Dad must have managed to fulfil his promise to buy her a camera and she used it to snap pictures of us at every opportunity. I wonder if this was prompted by a deep rooted fear of losing her children. She had no photos of Bertie, Audrey and Noel and must have wanted to make sure that if anything happened to us she would have our images on record.

I once came across an old cardboard box with many small packets of undeveloped films: the hundreds of photos of us that Mum took but could not afford to have developed. I am surprised that she managed to afford to have as many of the films developed as she did. Most of the photos have now been lost but there are enough there to demonstrate what must have bordered on an obsession for my mother.

While Mum snapped photos of new additions to the family, Dad celebrated by singing and whistling. He was always delighted at the prospect of being a father again. I found out later from my brothers that he was ecstatic when I, his first daughter, came along. Apparently he went around for days whistling and singing *Jeannie with the Light Brown Hair*. I never did find out how I came to be called June and not

Jean. After me, came the twins which gave my father further cause for pride and jubilation.

He was just as excited about the expected arrival of his sixth child. He often lifted his old navy beret from his head, threw it into the air and caught it on the way down yelling, "I'm gonna be a dad. I'm gonna be a father again."

My mother's reaction was understandably more restrained. Each pregnancy would have stirred the ghosts of sorrow: memories of her first three pregnancies and the loss of those children. This must have dulled the joy of anticipation and added to the physical burden of pregnancy and childbirth. I think she also felt the weight of financial hardship.

She would sigh and say, "Another mouth to feed."

Apart from money worries, Mum still had the stress of having to cope on her own for up to two weeks at a stretch each time my father went out to the woodcutters' camp. The absence of a husband who wrapped her in love and warmth and cherished her with unabashed abandon must have added a sharp edge to her isolation.

Although financial commitment to his family was limited by circumstances, Dad's emotional commitment was seemingly endless. He loved being with Mum and did all he could to spend time with his family. One of my favourite memories is evening picnics on the Snowy River. Dad would catch a few big bream with a simple fishing line, scale and gut them and cook them directly on the hot coals of our fire; a truly delicious meal.

He taught us what to do if we encountered a snake in the bush and showed my brothers how to chop wood and fell trees. He was patient when he encouraged us to climb up on the back of our old draught horse Nugget for bareback rides around the yard. Old Nugget used to be part of a team of horses that helped haul logs out of the forest.

Drives through the bush were regular family outings. Dad stopped along the way to allow us to explore creek beds and climb trees and to teach us what he knew about the bush; pointing out various trees so that we learned to recognise a yellow stringybark from a mahogany or a messmate. Sometimes he took us out to the bush after a bushfire. An empty and silent forest greeted us. The scorched black ground was bare of scrub, dried leaves and undergrowth which had been burnt away. In the stillness, a battlefield of leafless trees stood like tall black sentinels. From time to time smoke sizzled from smouldering cinders on the ground but apart from that there was no sound and no forest smells.

Bushfires were pretty much an annual event in

the Orbost area. Fires often raced through the forests around the town. Our home out on the Bonang, being surrounded by bush, was in a dangerous position. Just prior to bushfire season, Dad, with the help of some of the woodcutters, conducted controlled burns, known as burning off, in the strip of forest that bordered our paddock as well as the bush along Duggans Road.

It was not unusual, in the summer, to see billowing clouds of smoke on the horizon or rising above the tree tops. The sight of fires sweeping along the hills was a source of delight for us kids. We were fascinated by the smell of burning eucalypts and the changing red and orange colours of the flames. In fact, Maxie and I were so inspired by the fires we witnessed that one year we won first and second prize in a school art competition for our paintings of fires, even though neither of us had demonstrated any particular artistic talent before.

Despite our poverty, Dad sometimes bought each of us a small treat (usually the cheapest available chocolate bars) when he made a trip into the township of Orbost. He would usually buy at least one bag of lollies such as Minties which he kept aside to be shared around over a period of several weeks. He sometimes gave me an extra lolly when the boys were not around. He would wink at me as he offered it to me and say, "Don't tell your mother." Mum did not like us eating too many lollies.

"Lollies are bad for your teeth," she used to say. "Why do you need lollies when we've got fresh fruit growing on trees?"

I doubt that Dad kept these 'secret' treats from my mother. I think it was just his way of making me feel special. He succeeded. I adored my father. No, I idolised my father. Although he was the symbol of authority in our family, he was, at the same time, the one who initiated fun, laughter and adventure. When he was away working in the bush I missed him terribly. I have no doubt that this was what caused me, one day when I was around six years old, to allow myself to be lured into one of the most dangerous situations a child could face.

It was a weekend and my two older brothers had, probably as a result of stern instructions from Mum to include their little sister, taken me with them on one of their regular jaunts to the local rubbish tip. I rode in the cart that Bobby had on the back of his bike. On the return journey it would be filled with various bits and pieces but I would find a crevice to squeeze my skinny body into.

We trundled along the highway and turned into the track that led to the area in the bush that had been set aside for the locals to dump their rubbish.

The steamy smell of fermenting organic matter coalesced with the bracing scent of eucalyptus. When we arrived, I hopped out of the cart and ran toward the entwined piles of twisted metal, garden scraps, broken furniture, children's unwanted toys and other assorted and 'assaulted' junk. Bobby leant his bike against a tree. Maxie's bike fell to the ground and lay sideways, one wheel still spinning as he raced his brother to the waiting trash. We were all tense with excitement at the thought of potential treasures waiting to be found. My brothers whooped and yelled whenever they found a piece of machinery or bits of old cars.

"Hey! Look what I found."

"I found a whole steering wheel. Look!"

They examined and compared each other's discoveries. Some items were thrown back onto the piles of rubbish and some were carefully placed in the cart. I searched only for books. I always found some. It never ceased to amaze me that people could be so rich as to afford to throw books away; 'perfectly good books' as my mother would say.

There was one other person there that day. He was a little distance away from us picking his way through the rubbish. When I first noticed him, I stopped what I was doing and made to walk toward him because, for an instant, I thought he was my father. He wore similar work clothes, with sleeves rolled up over brown muscular arms. He had the same thick black hair and his face was, so it seemed to me, the same dark brown as my father's deeply suntanned face. Something stopped me from going to him; perhaps the rational part of my brain acknowledged that if he were my father, Bobby and Maxie would have recognised him. Yet when the man turned, possibly noticing my movement, and fixed his dark brown eyes on me, I saw my dad's eyes and I projected my father's features onto the man's face. He smiled at me. Part of me was sure he was the father whom I was missing dreadfully because he had been away working in the bush for over a week.

As I lost myself in my illusion about the man, I became less aware of my brothers who continued their noisy discoveries. The man gradually moved closer to me. I was mesmerised. I wanted so much for him to be Dad. He said nothing but smiled at me from time to time as he picked over bits of rubbish. My brothers moved further away, determined not to overlook any new piles of rubbish that might have arrived since their last visit to the tip. I had already found several books. Clutching them to my chest, I concentrated on watching the man who was my father and yet was not my father.

When my brothers called to me, their voices reached my ears as though from far away.

"Come on, June."

I ignored them.

"Come on. We're going now."

I could not leave this man. I could not bear the thought of being separated from him. He had his back to my brothers and seemed to be still sifting through rubbish but he inclined his head in my direction, smiled and spoke softly.

"Want to ride on my bike?"

I nodded. My brothers had mounted their bikes and rode over to us.

"Hop in the cart," Bobby said to me. "We're going home now."

I said nothing.

"All right," said Maxie. "We'll leave you here if you don't get in the cart in five seconds."

They both counted.

"One. Two."

This was a technique Mum sometimes used when we refused to comply with her instructions. We had to obey by the time she counted to five – 'or else'. She rarely had to count all the way to five before we gave her complete obedience. In my case, she rarely made it past the number two.

My brothers turned their bikes to face the track

exit.

"Three. Four. You'll get into trouble if you don't come with us."

They started to pedal.

"Five."

I stayed where I was. My brothers rode along the track slowly. When they realised I was not coming, they increased their pedalling to normal speed and left the rubbish tip. I didn't care. I felt completely safe with the man I had momentarily replaced my father with. He smiled at me.

Chapter 7

I WAITED, WATCHING HIS MUSCULAR arms while he examined a few more items. Then he stood up, took my hand and led me to where his bicycle was leaning against a tree. He lifted me up and placed me in the basket that was attached to the front handle bars. I sat there, still clutching my books, with my legs dangling over the edge of the basket while he held the bicycle steady and swung one leg over the seat. His strong legs pedalled the bike along the track and out onto the Bonang Highway in the direction of the town and my home.

I couldn't have been happier. It was as though my longing for my father had been fulfilled by a fairy godmother. A prince had ridden in from a fairy tale and rescued me from my rough, unsympathetic brothers. I was the favoured princess being given exclusive privileges. With smug satisfaction I settled back in the basket and breathed in the tobacco smell coming from the man which was the same as my father's tobacco smell. Parrots chattered and kooka-burras cackled and the bike's wheels crunched through the gravel and soft yellow dirt by the side of the road. A short distance along the highway, the man stopped his bicycle and dismounted.

"We gotta go up there for a minute."

He pointed at a dirt track. It was not a road but a track made by the vehicles of the woodcutters who went deep into the bush to fell trees.

This was even more exciting for me. An extra adventure! He wheeled the bicycle, with me still in its basket, along the bush track. A breeze whistled through the leaves of the tall eucalypts. Parrots chattered high above us. A startled lizard scampered across the dry leaves on the ground.

When the man stopped and propped the bike against a tree, some primal instinct sent a warning to my brain. I felt uncertain. I looked back along the track but could not see the highway. We were in the bush. The man who was not my father lifted me out of the basket and set me down on the ground. The warning signal that had reached my child brain began to ring like a school bell. Tears rolled down my cheeks. The distant sound of a car engine floated over the tree tops. The man cast a nervous glance back toward the highway. I cried silently. He bent down toward me.

"Don't cry," he said in his soft voice. "I won't hurt you."

I hesitated, wanting to believe his words. I had no rational understanding of why I was crying. In my child mind I had no reason to distrust him.

"I only wanted to play with this," he said as he slipped his fingers inside the leg of my panties and touched the soft area between my legs.

The murmur of the car engine changed as though the car was slowing down. The man withdrew his fingers and looked around nervously again. Then he picked me up and placed me once more in the bike basket. He wheeled the bike along the track back to the highway where he mounted the bicycle and resumed pedalling toward town. I had stopped crying but I was confused, not sure what had just happened. I had now removed the illusion that the man was my father but he had been gentle. He had kept his promise; he had not hurt me. Now he was taking me home. Everything seemed normal. I was with an adult who was looking after me.

Meanwhile back at home, as I found out later from my brothers, Bobby and Maxie were receiving a wrathful scolding from our mother. She was aghast when they returned from the tip without me.

"You left her there?"

"She wouldn't come with us."

"So you just left her there to walk home on her own?"

"She won't have to walk. There was a man there with a bike."

"Yeah. He'll probably give her a ride home."

"A man? Who?"

"Dunno. A blackfella."

I can only imagine the fear that would have surged through my mother as she listened to my brothers casually relate how they had left me at the rubbish tip with a stranger. She must have exercised a great deal of discipline to keep that fear and, no doubt, her anger from translating into panic. Her tone was sharp as she admonished my brothers.

"How many times have I told you about not speaking to strangers? Yet you go and leave your sister there with a stranger?"

My brothers later told me they had 'never seen her so mad'. 'Her eyes were like a tiger's.' Faced with the urgent problem of finding me, Mum didn't waste time in punishing them at that moment. She rapped out orders at them.

"You two stay here and look after the babies. Do you hear me? You stay here. Keep an eye on those babies. If anything happens to either of them while I'm gone your lives won't be worth living when your father gets home."

Bobby and Maxie had already realised that they were in line for a 'jolly good hiding' when Dad got home. They were smart enough not to do anything to make it worse. Both of them searched their brains desperately for something that might put them back in Mum's good books.

"I think it was Jacky, Mum," said Maxie.

"Yeah. It looked like Jacky, Mum. He's not a stranger, is he?"

Jacky was an Aboriginal man, one of the local Kurnai people, who often worked in the bush with my father and the other timber workers. His wife, Lizzie, would sometimes bring their children, two boys and three girls, out to our place when the men were away working. We would all play together while Mum and Lizzie sat and drank cups of tea.

"Good for your Junie to have some girls to play with for a change, eh?" Lizzie would say.

Mum liked Lizzie and her children. She loved the way Lizzie's kids flashed big cheeky grins at her.

"Your kids are always so happy, Lizzie," she would say.

Lizzie would puff up with pride and nod her head.

"Naughty little varmints, that's what they are," she'd say, "but, yeah, they're happy so I don't mind. So long as they're happy, eh?"

The thought that I might be with Jacky or some-one else we knew may have given my mother some relief but she continued to glare at my brothers.

"For your sakes, it'd better be someone we know," she said. "And you'd better hope she hasn't gone off on her own and got lost in the bush."

With no phone and no vehicle, walking back to the rubbish tip herself offered the best course of action to Mum even though she was six months pregnant. She could have gone to our neighbours at the dairy a kilometre away but that might have wasted time; she could not be sure of finding some-one there with a vehicle.

As she hurried along Duggans Road to the high-way that day Mum must have been hoping that it had been Lizzie's husband at the tip and, thinking I would be safe with him, that he had decided to bring me home on his bike. She might also have wondered, though, why Jacky hadn't simply made sure my brothers took me home with them.

Jacky and I were less than a kilometre from home when Mum saw us. She stopped and waited, her hand resting on her swollen stomach. As the distance between us closed, I could see the tension in her face. A half smile appeared, perhaps because she recog-nised Jacky. Her eyes were on me as Jacky braked and put a foot on the ground to stop the bike. With the uncanny intuition of a mother, Mum saw something in my face that caused her half smile to disappear.

"Are you all right, love?" she said.

"Yes, Mum. I got some books from the tip." Afraid that I would get into trouble for not going with my brothers or for what had happened with Jacky, I wanted desperately to distract her.

"Did you, love?" Her eyes were gentle as she looked into mine. I was too young to know that eyes can reveal much so I did not take evasive action by looking away or lowering my eyelids. My mother apparently saw enough to know that nothing dreadful had happened to me but that something was not quite right.

"Jacky, what are you doing with my daughter?" She said as she helped me out of the basket and set me down. I could not see the look in her eyes but the tone of her voice revealed her suspicion.

"Bringin' her home to you, missus. Those brothers, they left her there, left her at the rubbish tip. Too far for little girl to walk, missus."

I heard apprehension in Jacky's voice.

"I think you had better go, Jacky," said my mother.

Jacky rode off on his bicycle. Mum and I walked home. She never said another word to me about that day.

I was surprised when I did not receive a scolding or a hiding for not going home with my brothers. Even though my naivety prevented me from fully understanding why, I knew that what Jacky had done was wrong. However, I saw myself as the guilty one and was determined that my mother should not find out so I never spoke about it. The incident became just another adventure in long days full of adventures. It wasn't until years later when a friend from high school days mentioned Jacky's name that my memory opened up its album of pictures and showed them to me as bright and clear as the day it had happened. I also discovered that the town kids knew Jacky was a 'perve'.

I don't think my mother discussed her suspicions about Jacky with Lizzie. How could she, after all? However, she must have been concerned for Lizzie's daughters because one day she dropped a hint. Mum and Lizzie were sitting on the veranda where they always sat. I was at the end of the veranda playing 'knuckle bones' with Poppy, one of Lizzie's daughters who was the same age as me. I pricked up my ears when I heard my name mentioned.

"Junie still miss her father when he's away?" asked Lizzie.

"Yes, she pines for him like a puppy pines for its

mother."

I heard Lizzie's rich laugh. There was a pause before my mother spoke again.

"Her father's very good with her. Some men are not good with their daughters. And Lizzie…"

My mother paused again. A subtle change in her tone caught my attention. I looked over at them.

"Some fathers," continued Mum, "can be…"

She broke off. Lizzie looked across at her. Mum didn't turn to look at her. Instead she stared out at the bush.

"Well," continued my mother, "sometimes they can be too friendly with their daughters."

Lizzie turned away, cradled her cup of tea in her hands and also looked out at the bush. The two women sat in silence.

"Too friendly," said Lizzie finally. "Yeah, I know whatcha mean. We have to look after our girls, eh?"

As she placed her cup back down on the saucer, Lizzie looked over and caught me eagerly digesting their conversation. Her face broke out in a broad grin.

"Whatcha doin', you two? Listenin' to grown-up talk? Haven't ya got better things to be doin'?"

Poppy and I giggled, gathered up our knuckle bones, joined hands and ran away with the laughter of our mothers following us.

Knowing what I know now, I wonder if my 'adventure' brought thoughts of Myrtle's 'lost' children to her mind. Did she wonder about their safety? Did the guilt of not being there to protect them surge to the surface? Did she worry that Audrey, now a teenager, might need protection and advice?

Chapter 8

My mother's pregnancy resulted in the safe delivery of a healthy baby girl at Orbost Hospital in November, 1956. This time my father was singing *Goodnight Irene*. As with all his children, he enjoyed interacting with Irene from the beginning. He often held the baby in his arms and rocked her back and forth to put her to sleep or to soothe her.

Although Dad enjoyed tactile involvement as a proud father, Mum was definitely the expert with babies. I found her casual competence fascinating. When the twins were little, I was often with her when she was changing them. She needed me to keep one occupied while she attended to the other one. She would lay the baby out on a 'bunny rug', push up his little singlet and rub his tummy playfully to distract him while she undid the large safety pins on each side of his nappy. Then she would quickly remove the dirty nappy, fold it over and place it to one side. I loved the way she would lift up both his chubby legs in one hand, like a trussed chicken, and wipe his bottom with a damp cloth. If he was red and chafed she would rub Vaseline over his skin before lowering his bottom down onto a clean nappy.

The next step was to sprinkle talcum powder over the lower part of his body. Sometimes she allowed me to do this. All during this process Mum would keep the baby distracted by occasionally kissing his stomach, tweaking his nose or talking to him with her face close to his. The final step was the trickiest to manoeuvre because regardless of which twin it was, he hated having the new nappy put on. However, Mum folded up the corners of the nappy and deftly slipped the large safety pins through the folds of fabric before his protest had a chance to get into full swing.

I also helped her with other household chores. I don't remember her ever asking me to help. Being with her was a natural part of my life and she simply included me in what she was doing. Sometimes we would pick fruit from the trees in the orchard. Mum reincarnated this home grown fruit in various ways. She made fruit pies, bottled some of it, stewed some of it and made much of it into jam. I loved her plum jam because she always left the pips in. I enjoyed discovering them in the jam that I spread thickly over my bread, and sucking on them.

One job we all wanted to do for Mum was collecting the eggs from the chook house. We would fight to be the chosen one.

"Can I, Mum? Can I? Can I?"

"I wanna do it, Mum."

"It's my turn. You did it yesterday."

"I wanna do it."

Our chooks were good layers so what we did not need for our own use Mum exchanged for other foodstuffs such as milk from the dairy. Wrapping up the eggs was another job she did with casual ease. She wrapped each one individually and yet kept them together so that she ended up with a rectangular block of six eggs snugly enclosed in newspaper.

One Saturday morning about six months after Irene was born a new arrival of a different kind had my father in a state of excitement.

Saturdays and Sundays provided us kids with hours of adventure and wide open spaces to ramble. Apart from the thrill of visiting the rubbish tip, we had sheep to chase, rams to ride, blackberries and mushrooms to pick. We tried to entice rabbits out of their burrows and startled goannas out of hollow logs. Having the disadvantage of being a girl and younger than Bobby and Maxie, I was not always permitted to roam about the countryside.

On the Saturday morning of the new arrival, I was helping my mother in the vegetable garden. Mum's vegetable garden was extensive. Pumpkins sprawled all along a side fence, potatoes grew in profusion among the rows of peas and beans and tomatoes. She always had a large patch of rhubarb; a favourite vegetable of hers. The vegetable patch was actually a source of delight and discovery for us kids. We searched for hidden potatoes and watched to see how big the pumpkins would get. We especially loved eating fresh pea pods straight off the vine. Mum and I were picking peas on this day when the honking of a car horn interrupted us.

The twins, now almost five years old, were playing together close by. The two boys had evolved into very different individuals. Georgie was a serious child who hardly smiled and was inclined to be a little chubby while Kevin was slim and agile and radiated cheekiness with his dimpled smile. At the sound of the horn, the twins stopped playing.

"Car, Mum," said Kevin.

Mum smiled at him. She dropped a handful of pea pods into the pot that was already three quarters full of fresh green pods, then placed it in the shade behind the plants.

"Come on," she said. Like little ducklings, we all followed her as she started off toward the front of the house to see what was happening. The car horn sounded again as we rounded the corner of the house.

There in the driveway stood a large black saloon, its motor still running. Two headlights stuck out like overgrown ears on either side of the long bonnet snout. Standing by the open driver's door, with one foot on the running board, stood my father, his old navy beret cocked to one side on his head. A grin lit up his handsome, angular face. In that grin my mother might have seen remnants of the cheeky young soldier he had been when she first met him more than ten years before. He beamed at her, like a kid proud of procuring some treasure that he never thought he would find.

Behind my father stood his good friend Gus McCole, a gentle giant even taller than my father's six feet. Gus McCole was well known in the district as an expert axeman. He was held in high regard, not just for his legendary prowess with the axe, but because he was a man of sincerity, loyalty and integrity. Gus's kind eyes sparkled with merriment when he saw the look of surprise on my mother's face. I noticed Bobby and Maxie, who must have heard the car arrive, running across the green paddock next door.

"What is that?" my mother asked, her eyes fixed

on the car.

Dad and Gus threw back their heads and laughed. They looked like two little boys who had been up to mischief together. The twins ran to the vehicle. Kevin headed for the front of the car, leaning on the bumper and reaching up to try to touch a protruding headlight. Georgie watched his brother with a serious expression.

Dad stopped laughing to answer Mum. "This, Mrs Rowley, is your new car."

Mrs Rowley was a term of endearment he some-times used. In that title he proudly claimed her as his wife and declared his love for her.

Mum took a step back as though fearful for her life.

"My what?"

"Your new car. I want you to have some form of transport for when I'm out in the bush. You and the kids are too isolated here."

"But I can't drive this thing. I haven't driven in years."

"Don't worry. Once you're in the driver's seat it'll all come back to you. Eh, Gus?"

Gus, still grinning at Mum, nodded. "You'll pick it up in no time, Myrtle."

"I'll teach you how to drive this little baby," said Dad eagerly. He was always keen to instruct her in new skills.

"Teaching me is one thing but I'll need to get a licence."

"Of course you'll need a licence. But with me teaching you, you'll have your licence before you can say Jack Robinson."

Mum rolled her eyes in mock disbelief. "Where on earth did you get it? We can't afford a new car."

"It's not exactly new; it's a 1928 Erskine," said Dad. "And she won't cost us anything except registration and running expenses."

Mum widened her eyes in surprise.

"Gus found it lying around in a shed."

Gus laughed. "That's right, Myrtle. This old Erskine has been sitting around doing nothing for years. What earthly good is that? One of the best cars ever made, this little beauty. Might as well put her to good use, I reckon."

It was no surprise that the generous Gus McCole had come to our rescue. He and his wife Mavis were not well off and yet they were always ready to help anyone out.

Dad stepped back and gestured at the gleaming automobile. "Isn't she something?"

My mother's expression no doubt conveyed her opinion that it was just a black car. Seeing Kevin was attempting to climb up onto the front of it, Dad gently pulled him away. Gus stepped forward and hoisted Georgie up onto his shoulders. Bobby and Maxie arrived panting with exertion.

"Can we go for a ride?" they chorused.

Without waiting for an answer, they climbed into the back seat scrambling through separate doors in an attempt to beat each other inside.

"Come on, love. Hop into the driver's seat," said Dad.

Mum laughed and made no move toward the car.

Gus offered encouragement. "Go on. Take her for a spin."

Mum shook her head. "I'm the one who'll be in a spin."

Dad was not going to take no for an answer. His excitement about his new acquisition was infectious but Mum continued to eye the black vehicle thoughtfully. Despite her apprehension, she was no doubt considering the advantages of having a car to use while Dad was away. Dad sensed she was ready to yield.

"Come on, Mum. Just take her down to the gate. Get a feel for her."

He carried Kevin to the car.

"Let's put these two little tykes in the back with their brothers."

Georgie was struggling to get down so Gus lowered him to the ground and led him by the hand to a back passenger door. My father called to me over his shoulder.

"Come on, Brigid."

"They won't all fit into the back seat," said Mum with a laugh.

But we did. We squashed and prodded and leaned and squeezed and found room.

Mum made one final protest. "The baby's asleep on the veranda."

The most recent addition to our family was always called 'the baby' or, in the case of the twins, 'the babies', until a new baby arrived. This particular baby was my sister, Irene.

"Gus'll keep an eye on her. Won't you, Gus?"

Gus nodded. "Yeah. She'll be right as rain with me."

Finally, Mum admitted defeat and gave in with a smile and a shake of her head. Dad hurried over to her.

"Well," he said, gently steering her toward the open driver's side door. "What are we waiting for?"

Mum allowed him to lead her to the car. With some hesitation, she slid in behind the steering wheel. Dad closed the door, checked that both back doors were properly shut, opened the front passenger side door and got in. He turned to his brood of kids in the back seat and gave us a conspiratorial wink.

"Let's go for a drive," he said.

He slid across the bench seat closer to Mum. She fingered the steering wheel and looked at Dad with a twinkle in her eye.

"Well, what do I do now?" I could see she was beginning to enjoy herself.

Dad beamed at her. Patiently, he explained the function of the pedals and levers.

Mum released the handbrake. The car jumped forward. It rocked and lurched and hopped like a kangaroo. Mum laughed and eventually managed to settle the car into a smooth motion. Then, with Dad's confident hands on the steering wheel to guide her, she manoeuvred a turn so that we were heading toward the gate. The car rattled down the driveway. Dad grinned over at Gus who waved at us as we passed. Mum's hands gripped the steering wheel tightly.

"C'mon Mum, you're doing well. We'll take her along the track for a bit."

Mum was too absorbed in her task to answer. The car seemed to have a mind of its own.

"Slow her down a little as you go through the gate."

Mum looked at the controls, unsure what to do.

"Ease your foot off the throttle," he said.

She did as he instructed. The car slowed as it passed through the gateway. Dad's hands turned the steering wheel so that they made a right hand turn into Duggans Road. Turning left would have taken us up to the highway and my mother was definitely not ready for that. Surprisingly, the car rolled along the gravel road without hopping or jerking. Mum pressed her foot down gently on the throttle and we picked up speed slightly. Dad removed his hands from the steering wheel. Instinctively, Mum tightened her grip. He smiled and reassured her.

"It's all right, love. You're doing fine."

She nodded and seemed to relax.

Sitting in the back seat as we passed the trees on one side of the road and the green paddocks of the farm on the other, I tried to forget about my brothers fidgeting and squashing into me and imagined myself to be a grand dame on a country drive.

My daydream was interrupted by a sudden bump. The car seemed to leap into the air. We were heading towards the broad trunk of an old gum tree. The tree trunk was getting closer and closer. Mum's eyes were shut tight. Dad grabbed the steering wheel. I heard the sharp snapping of dry twigs under the car wheels. Bump! The car jumped and rocked. The engine died. We had stopped within inches of the broad gum tree.

"That was fun, Mum," said Bobby.

"Yeah. Can we do it again?" said Maxie.

Mum's hands were still gripping the steering wheel even though Dad had taken over the steering. She opened her eyes cautiously, then widened them at the sight of the tree in front of the windscreen. Dad removed his hands from the wheel. Mum looked across at him. He took off his beret and ran one hand through his thick black hair then returned her glance with a bemused smile. She grinned. Then she laughed. Her laugh was never far from the surface. As a child I did not realise laughter could be used as a release from tension or anxiety. Dad's smile widened to a grin.

"Well," he said. "We'd better get this old girl back on the road. I'll get out and crank her up."

"We can help, Dad," said Bobby.

"Not today, son," said Dad. "You kids stay where you are."

Bobby and Maxie looked crestfallen but they knew better than to argue with their father. While Dad was at the front of the car valiantly encouraging 'the old girl' to kick back into life with vigorous turns of the crank handle, Mum followed the various technical instructions he called to her. "Pull the choke out." "Foot on the throttle; gently." "Push the choke in a bit."

"Keep her ticking over," he called as the car sputtered and coughed out smoke through the exhaust. Finally, the motor kicked into life.

Bobby and Maxie cried, "Hooray!"

Mum slid across the seat to the passenger side. I guess she had had enough of driving for one day. Dad slipped into the driver's seat and looked across at Mum.

"That'll be the hardest thing for you to learn; using the crank handle."

"It certainly doesn't look easy."

"It'll be okay once you get the hang of it, love. Besides, Bobby's probably strong enough to do it for you."

"Yes. I can do it, Mum."

"Me too, Mum. I can help crank it," said Maxie.

Eventually, with my father's patient guidance, my mother learned to drive the Erskine. She could even manage the crank handle, but preferred Bobby or Maxie to do it.

I recall several unfortunate incidents over the years when my mother was at the wheel of the car. No one was ever injured although trees sometimes changed shape. Dad would survey the damage and simply scratch his head in amazement as though he thought Mum had achieved a remarkable feat in getting the car halfway up the trunk of a tree. They laughed these mishaps off, as they did with most calamities.

That's what our life was like; humorous incidents and dramatic events followed each other closely. Though financially poor, as a family we were rich in experiences that connected us. Everything revolved around the family. Our small two bedroom house overflowed with children who raced in and out of doorways, climbed through windows and up onto the roof, splashed along creek beds and ran wild across the green paddocks of the farm gleefully dispersing sheep and rabbits.

As our lives somersaulted on, we kids were completely oblivious to the existence of our three half-siblings elsewhere in Australia. My mother must have yearned to talk to someone about them. She must have wondered daily about how they were doing.

"During the years when my son was a baby, I used to look at other babies around his age and wonder how he was doing and what he looked like. These thoughts still continue today..." comments a mother whose child was taken from her at birth. (*Releasing the Past: Mothers' stories of their stolen babies*)

I think sometimes we must have reminded Mum of Bertie, Audrey and Noel because I occasionally observed a fleeting look in her eyes that I did not understand at the time, that seemed out of place in the context. Perhaps unseen ghosts from her past life caught her unawares.

Chapter 9

I WONDER IF MUM'S HABIT of nurturing everything she could find resulted, at least in part, from the loss of her first three children. She always seemed to have some young creature in her care. In the spring she would walk around the paddocks next door and check for lambs that needed mothering. When ewes had multiple births, they would sometimes reject the extra lambs. Mum would gather the orphaned lambs and the lambs of sick ewes and bottle feed them. Sometimes she would bring a weak lamb inside and make a cosy bed for it in an old cardboard box and keep it near the stove where it would be warm. Actually, I think the young sheep quickly caught on that Mum was a soft touch because the group of woolly white lambs jostling each other for her attention often included those that did not need a surrogate mother.

On occasion, a sick lamb might share the warmth of the stove with a box of fluffy yellow chickens.

These were my favourites. My mother kept them in an old shoe box with holes in the lid which she placed near the stove. For chickens that had just hatched, Mum positioned their shoebox on one of the side bricks, part of the hearth in which the stove was set, where it was warmest.

Mum loved birds of any kind and delighted in watching the tiny blue wrens, robin red breasts and little grey thrushes that often flew into her garden. If she found a bird with a broken leg or wing she would try to nurse it back to health. She taught us to distinguish one bird from the other, especially the difference between a sparrow and a starling. In those days we had slingshots. Mum did not want us to mistakenly shoot sparrows thinking they were starlings. The only birds she would allow us to shoot at were starlings because they were pests. She usually had a pet bird, sometimes a canary and at other times a blue budgerigar. It seems to me the budgies were always called Bluey. As far as I can remember, Mum did not give the new budgies new names.

She also loved dogs and most other animals. However, one creature Mum did not show much affection for was the snake. She was afraid of them, as were most people in Australia at that time. 'The only good snake is a dead snake' was a mantra often heard. Snakes in the bush were part of our lives and

Dad had taught us not to touch, catch or try to kill them. We came across snakes several times when we were gathering wood for the fire. I recall one occasion when we saw a black snake curled up under a log.

"Stand still," said Dad, keeping his eyes on the reptile while holding one arm out to block Bobby, Maxie and me from moving forward.

He slowly reached up to his fedora hat which sometimes replaced the well worn navy beret, took it off and carefully lowered it before finally letting it fall to the ground between him and the snake.

We stood perfectly still and quiet behind Dad. I used my father's legs as a shield while my brothers held their bodies slightly to the side so that they could see the snake.

"Move backwards slowly," said Dad.

I kept my eyes closed as we inched backwards. My heart was pounding.

"It's moving," hissed Bobby.

I gripped my father's trouser leg.

"It's gonna get us," said Maxie.

"Shh," said Dad.

When Dad stopped moving backwards, we all stopped. I tried to shut my eyes even tighter as I imagined the snake's gleaming black body slithering towards us. I couldn't understand why we had stopped moving. I wanted to run – very fast.

"It's gone," said Maxie.

I didn't open my eyes. I did not trust my brothers. Maxie might be playing a trick on me.

"All right," said Dad. "You can relax now."

I opened my eyes at last. Bobby made to move toward Dad's hat but Dad put a restraining hand on him.

"Careful," he said.

He picked up a long branch and poked at the hat, lifting it up and reeling it in like a fish on a line.

"Come on," said Dad. "We have enough wood for now."

We carefully gathered up our bundles of dry sticks that Mum called morning wood, probably because she used it to light the fire in the morning, and returned home.

Snakes in the bush were one thing. Having snakes around the house was a different matter altogether. Any of us kids could easily be bitten, either by accidentally treading on a snake or because of our own foolishness. Besides, snakes had been known to venture into people's houses. So when my brothers discovered a nest of slim, silver baby snakes under the wooden platform at the end of the veranda on which the rainwater tank stood, Dad had to do something. I watched the writhing bundle of hatchlings with revulsion. From the look on my mother's face, she apparently felt the same. She gathered all of us up onto the veranda. Bobby and Maxie protested but she was firm.

"Let your father handle it," she said.

Dad pushed his hat back and scratched his head.

"I can get rid of these hatchlings easily enough," he said. "But I'm worried there might be an adult around somewhere."

He used a long pole to lift the loose timber and rocks under the water tank, keeping his distance lest a snake dart out and strike at him. Eventually he satisfied himself that there were no adult snakes hiding anywhere.

"All right, Bobby and Max, you can come and help me now," said Dad.

My brothers were down from the veranda like a shot.

"Keep your eyes peeled and yell if you see an adult snake," he said.

He then used a shovel to drag the bundle of baby snakes from under the tank-stand out into the open where he could kill them. By now the full realisation of what had to happen to the hatchlings must have hit Mum.

"Dad," she said, before my father even had a chance to raise the shovel to strike.

He looked at her.

"They're only babies," she said.

He shook his head. "We can't leave them, Mum. It's too dangerous."

She didn't say anything else but held his eyes. Something passed between them. Finally, Dad nodded.

"Max," he said. "Go and fetch me a hessian bag from the shed. Bobby, keep your eyes peeled for that snake."

So, while Mum took the rest of us inside the house, Dad, with help from my brothers, bagged the baby snakes. Later, he took the squirming bag out into the bush.

I don't remember seeing my father kill any snakes but my brothers did. They recounted one slaying with emphasis on the gruesome details.

"Dad just whacked it on the head with the shovel," said Bobby.

"Hard," said Maxie. "He whacked it hard."

"Yeah, its tail was flicking around like crazy."

"You shoulda seen it. Dad just kept whacking 'til it was dead."

"Dead as a doornail."

Chapter 10

EVEN MY FATHER COULD NOT overcome the calamity that arrived in 1958. Because of my habit of eavesdropping on my parents, I was the first of the kids to know about it.

One night when I was supposed to be in bed I was crouched underneath the half open window of the kitchen, part of which was now converted to my bedroom after all the meals for the day were done with. I had an excellent vantage point for listening. On the other side of the window, my parents sat on the veranda playing cards in the light of the kerosene lantern. This was a favourite past time of theirs and they taught us kids to play games like Euchre and Five Hundred. But when their labours were done and the kids were all finally in bed, they enjoyed some time together. This particular night I heard my mother quizzing my father about his uncharacteristic tiredness. He then admitted to other symptoms of possible illness.

"There's blood," he said, "when I go to the toilet."

There was a short silence before my mother responded.

"Well, you'd better get yourself off to the doctor, hadn't you?"

My father, who was usually the one to give Mum strength, would not have admitted his symptoms to her like that unless he sensed something was seriously wrong.

"The sooner they find out what it is, the sooner they'll be able to treat you. You're as strong as an ox. You'll be better in no time," she said.

"I hope so, love." His tone was serious.

Later that week, my father went to the doctor who gave him a thorough examination and took a blood sample to be sent to Melbourne for testing. My parents then had to wait for the results of the tests.

When the results arrived, the doctor telephoned our house. It was one of those lazy days that uncurl slowly like a koala waking from a deep sleep. My mother was in the yard feeding the chooks. The boys were off somewhere playing. I was sitting on the verandah step minding two-year-old Irene. A gentle sun warmed our bodies. The day's tranquillity was terminated by a shrill ringing from inside the house.

The phone had been installed when Pop became ill. My father, with a little help from my grandmother, Olive, managed to scrape up the money needed. It was a heavy black contraption which scared the daylights out of me. My parents did not use the phone on a regular basis because of the expense. It was primarily for my grandmother to call Dad if she needed him.

The sound of the black Bakelite monster echoed through the house. I got up and went into the kitchen where the telephone sat, squat and fat on an old dresser. I stared at the instrument but it was no longer ringing. As I turned to go back outside, it blasted its tune again. I jumped in startled surprise and fear before running out onto the veranda. In the distance, I could see my mother scooping seeds from her ballooned apron and scattering them around near the chook house. A flock of pecking hens surrounded her. I called out.

"Muu…um! Muu…um!"

Her head turned toward the house. Another shrill ring came from inside. I called again with more urgency in my voice.

"Muu…um!"

She called back. "What's the matter?"

"It's ringing! It's ringing, Mum."

She laughed. "Pick it up then. Quick, love. I'll be right there."

Mum emptied her apron, brushed the remaining

seeds from it and hurried toward the house. I went back into the kitchen and tentatively reached for the black handset, hesitating before placing my hand on it, afraid the loud shrill sound would blast from it again. Then I pounced on it and quickly picked it up and held it to my ear, the way my father had showed me when he had demonstrated how to use it. I listened and waited. Nothing. I pressed it harder up against my ear straining to hear. Suddenly a booming male voice crackled through the handset and frightened me.

"Hello?" the voice said.

I dropped the handset and ran from the room, colliding with my mother as she hurried along the veranda and into the kitchen to the telephone.

The doctor explained he had the results of the blood tests and would like to see Dad to discuss them. Mum could glean no clues from his friendly but professional tone.

The day Dad came back from town after seeing the doctor he announced that he had to go to Melbourne for more tests.

"They seem to think I might have some sort of blood disorder," he said. "I told the doc there was nothing wrong with my blood; good blood. Rowley blood, I told him. But he wasn't having it; thinks it might be serious. They want me to report to the

Alfred Hospital next Friday."

Mum did not know what to say.

"Could be a virus," she said.

"Yeah," Dad smiled ruefully. "That's what the doctor said. It could be just a virus; some sort of new virus upsetting the balance of blood cells, or something like that."

Mum smiled hopefully.

Dad decided to drive down to Melbourne on the day of his appointment at the Alfred Hospital, setting off around two in the morning. We all went. It was too far for Dad to drive on his own as he was not well, although he protested that he was 'perfectly all right'. Mum could not go with him unless we went too. They packed us into the back of the truck and set off. Dad had rigged up a makeshift canopy over the tray at the back to make a mobile bedroom, with blankets and pillows from our beds. Mum nursed my sister Irene on her lap in the cabin.

Dad knew the way well. We had made many trips to the Alfred Hospital before with my brother Kevin (one of the twins) who had epilepsy and suffered with sudden and severe convulsions.

I'll never forget the first time I saw him having a fit. He lay on the kitchen floor, his head yanked back by an invisible force. His thin body jerked up and down as though in response to sudden electrical shocks. Legs kicked. Arms flailed. Eyes rolled upward. Lips turned blue. His breathing sounded like a dentist's suction hose. White froth spilled out of his open mouth.

My mother ran to him and tried to hold his head still. "Get me a pillow," she yelled, "and a blanket."

We all stood around gaping, my three other brothers and me.

"Quickly," yelled my mother. Panic warped her voice to an unrecognisable screech.

I ran as fast as my eight-year-old legs could carry me, grabbed a blanket and pillow from my parents' bed, ran back and dropped them on the floor next to Mum. She deftly slipped the pillow under my brother's head and draped the blanket over him. All the while, his body continued to jerk like a crazy, robotic machine.

When he was quiet, my mother carried him to his bed and made sure he was warm. He slept for hours afterward.

Mum had become very efficient in handling Kevin's sudden seizures. On instructions from the doctor, she always had a soft wooden peg handy to place in his mouth lest he start to swallow his tongue. He had such an angelic face, it was weird and frightening to see it distorted and grotesque during his fits.

Our journey to Melbourne was not easy. Much of the road was bumpy and the springs in the truck's seat that were threatening to push through the upholstery would have made the trip uncomfortable for my parents. Added to this discomfort was the noise coming from the back where their non-angelic kids were not sleeping. Dad made regular stops to reprimand us. Each time he stopped, he was bombarded with complaints.

"Maxie keeps rolling over onto my blanket."

"She keeps moving around and waking everyone up." ('She' was the way my brothers referred to me when they were annoyed with me – which was most of the time.)

"Bobby snores."

"Kevin lets off poot poots," said Georgie.

Kevin giggled.

"And they stink," added Georgie.

When Dad had finally had enough of the frequent stopping to adjudicate our squabbles he used his sternest tone to threaten us.

"One more peep," he said, shining the torch on us. "One more peep out of any of you and I'll have the strap around your legs."

This was met with subdued silence from inside the back of the truck.

"Do you hear me?" he roared.

None of us spoke. With eyes on the belt around his waist, we nodded our heads, intimidated by his tone and his threat.

"Now lie down, all of you."

We obeyed meekly.

"And I don't care who is bumping into who. You can't expect to be sleeping in the back of a truck and not have someone bumping into you. It's not the Ritz you know."

He waited until we all settled back with our blankets curled around our thin bodies, eyes closed feigning deep and peaceful sleep. His anger, which was exaggerated for optimum effect, subsided as quickly as it had come. When he was satisfied we had settled, he pulled the canopy down and tied the ropes. We heard his footsteps returning to the cabin, heard the door open and bang shut. Then the truck began to move again.

It was shortly after dawn when we reached the outskirts of the city. Dad pulled the truck over to the side of the road and cut the engine. I heard my mother's voice, groggy from slumber.

"Get some sleep," she urged. "I've been sleeping most of the way. I'm fine now. I'll keep an eye on the kids."

He slept in the driver's seat stretching out his long legs as best he could. There was no sound from the back; my brothers were all asleep. The bush was quiet except for an occasional rustle in the under-growth. I peeped through a hole in the canopy and could just make out the outline of dark trees. Hours passed while I watched the darkness of night merging into morning light as my mother must have done. Once, Mum quietly eased herself out of the cabin and crept stealthily around to the back to peek through the gaps in the canopy to check on us. She would have seen me apparently fast asleep.

When shafts of light streaked through the trees and kookaburras and magpies called through the leaves, Mum woke Dad. I heard his boots scrunching the twigs and leaves underneath as he strode into the trees to relieve himself. When he returned, he opened up the canopy and we all headed for the trees while Dad cranked the truck back to life. Once we were all safely back in the truck, the last leg of our journey began.

I cannot remember what we did while Dad was in the hospital. I assume poor Mum tried to keep us occupied and under control in the park across the road. No doubt she had sandwiches and thermos flasks of water.

On the way home, I remember Dad saying to Mum, "They don't know what's wrong with me, love."

He sounded as though the weight of the world was on his shoulders. Mum said nothing.

There were to be more trips to the Alfred Hospital and many more tests before my father's illness was diagnosed.

Chapter 11

APART FROM THE TRIPS TO the Alfred Hospital, my father's illness did not change our lives at first; the lives of us kids that is. At the weekends we got up to our usual mischief. During the week we, the five who were school age, attended Orbost North Primary School which was a three-kilometre walk.

Mum usually walked with us to the end of Duggans Road where it intersected with the highway. She issued strict instructions that we not walk on the road or in the State forest but through the trees that formed a border between farmland and the highway. The best part of going to school was getting there. Along the way we looked for tadpoles in ponds, frightened birds from their nests and indulged in other playful antics such as mooing at the cows that sometimes lingered along the fences. In some sections, the smell of fresh cow dung and wet hay followed us, as did the flies. Our backs were usually covered in a layer of these black insects. Slapping one another's back to cause a swarm of the pesky flies to scatter through the air was lots of fun.

At the time I gave no thought to what it was like for Mum after we went to school. Now, however, I do wonder how she fared on her own with just one small child for company and only the bush for a neighbour. She was safe from the *mrarts* that wandered the forest because, for the most part, they only appeared to Aboriginal people. But what about her own phantoms; the ghosts of the living? To me she seemed to be a happy, dedicated mother but of course I knew nothing of what she was hiding. '...to those around me I appear quite normal,' states Cheryl King who was forced to give up her child at birth. 'However, no-one knows the torment that I suffer regularly. There are so many nights that I go to bed to cry and secretly mourn the family I have lost.' *(Releasing the Past: Mothers' stories of their stolen babies)*

My mother's torment might have haunted her during the quiet daylight hours when my father was away and we were at school. Driving into town as a distraction was not an option even though she now had a car. The Erskine had been replaced, perhaps because of 'injuries' received when Mum was driving, by an old blue ute. The ute was used only when absolutely necessary. Mum and Dad did not have enough money to 'waste' petrol on driving the car around 'for no good reason'. Of course she would have been kept busy with housework, the garden and cooking, but her mind was not as occupied as it usually was. She corresponded regularly with her mother, cousins and aunts in Albury. Writing these letters must have stirred buried memories. Would she have been troubled by thoughts of what had happened to her in Albury? To ensure the past did not bear down on her, she might have kept herself busy reading the short stories and serials in women's magazines and listening to the wireless. I know she always stopped at lunch time to listen to a fifteen minute radio soap opera broadcast on the ABC called *Blue Hills*.

I think Mum looked forward to our visits to Nan and Pop. The Sundays that Dad was at home we usually went into Orbost to have a roast dinner with our grandparents. Mum must have missed the companionship she enjoyed with her cousins in Albury and the close relationship she had with her mother. With Nan, she could share some of her experiences as a mother and perhaps seek her advice.

Nan and Pop had once owned a dairy farm but by this time they were living in Salisbury Street, Orbost. Nan was short, fat and round and she enchanted us kids. She increased our fascination by telling us she had 'Gypsy' blood and relating all sorts of exotic stories about faraway places. Pop, who had spent solitary days on the road as a drover, was quiet, thin and gentle. He seemed to spend a lot of time sitting in his favourite chair or pottering about in the shed. In my memory, Pop was always an old man but Nan said he had been a very handsome young man with wavy black hair and Valentino eyes when she met him. (Rudolph Valentino was a sex symbol of the silent movies who apparently had dark, smouldering eyes.) According to Nan, all the girls were after Pop but his smouldering eyes were firmly fixed on her.

It was not just Mum who looked forward to seeing Nan and Pop. We all loved going to their place for Sunday dinner, which was a midday meal as lunch was called dinner in those days. Nan and Mum cooked the meal together in Nan's kitchen which was at the rear of the house at one end of the back verandah. The kitchen had cupboards along one wall and a heavy wooden table pushed up against another. A long bench with a sink was strategically placed along the opposite wall where a window overlooked the side path. Anyone using the path to come to the house, which was almost everyone because the front door was rarely used, would be spotted immediately by Nan who spent a lot of her time at the kitchen bench. The bench stopped short of the remaining wall leaving a corner with enough space for a chair: Pop's big old comfortable chair. On cold nights Pop always had the best seat in the house because it was right by the open fire. Next to the fireplace was the large wood stove where the meals were cooked and which always had a kettle of water keeping warm at the back.

Although the table in the kitchen was used for most meals, we had Sunday roast in the 'formal dining room'. I thought this room, with its large fireplace and tall bay windows, very grand. Nan's best china was displayed in a walnut cabinet with glass doors. A gleaming mahogany table occupied pride of place in the centre of the room. A fat round ceramic vase bursting with freshly cut hydrangeas, their full round heads verifying Nan's skills as a gardener, sat on the table. This piece of antique furniture that had been handed down through generations of Nan's family, had an extension leaf. Its mystical ability to change size was a source of fascination for me and my siblings. We all gathered around to watch as Dad opened the table, unfolded the hidden panel and clicked it into place. Our eyes gleamed with delight to see the oval table magically transformed into what seemed to us to be a majestic banquet table. Sunday dinner was as grand as the room: roast lamb with gravy, potatoes, pumpkin and peas followed by jelly and cream.

The day Pop died my grandmother came out to our place in a taxi to tell us the news. It was January 1959, less than a year after my father's first trip to the Alfred Hospital. January that year recorded temperatures as high as 107.8 degrees (42.11 Celsius) in East Gippsland. Consequently, Orbost was surrounded by bushfires. In fact, the township itself had been under threat by a fire that jumped the Snowy River. Fire had wiped out thousands of acres of bush. Forest fires were burning around our place on the Bonang. It was not until mid February that the fire danger began to pass.

Pop's death was not unexpected because he had been ill for several years but that did not make it any easier for Nan. They had been a good match and Pop had been an excellent husband and father. Nan would miss him.

Not long after Pop died, Nan told Dad she did not want to live on her own.

"There's no reason why you and Myrtle and the kids can't move in with me, George," she said.

Dad nodded. He knew his mother was not really concerned about living on her own; it was his situation she was thinking of.

"Are you sure that's what you want, Mum?"

"What am I going to do with the extra rooms?"

said Nan. "Besides, I'd be grateful for Myrtle's company and a bit of help around the house."

Nan smiled across at my mother.

"You won't have much room if my brood moves in with you, Mum."

"We'll all fit in here just fine."

My mother laughed. "The kids'll drive you crazy."

Nan smiled. "Let me worry about that, Myrtle love. The way things are you'll be much better off here in town with me. I would have suggested it sooner but you know how poorly Pop has been. It wouldn't have been fair on him, or you and the kids for that matter, to have you move in while he was ill."

Mum nodded her understanding.

"I know George worries about you," Nan continued. "And so do I, out there on your own with the kids when he's away. Worrying about his family won't help him get over his illness."

Mum tilted her head and threw a teasing look at Dad.

"Oh, you don't need to worry about him, Mum. He's as strong as a Mallee bull. He'll be back to his old self in no time."

My grandmother smiled.

"Of course he will. He's always been strong and

healthy. The doctors'll sort him out as soon as they work out what it is; some new fangled virus no doubt. But for the time being they want him to do lighter work, don't they?"

Mum nodded.

"No work, more like it," said Dad with a dismissive laugh. "Honestly, these doctors must think a bloke's made of money; wanting me to lie around all day doing nothing."

Mum and Nan exchanged smiles at the thought of Dad with nothing to do.

"Well, anyway," said Nan. "Light work and doctors' appointments will be much easier to manage if you're with me here in Orbost and if you have to go back to the Alfred Hospital you won't have to worry about Myrtle and the kids. Besides, it'll be good for me; stop me fretting for Pop."

And so the decision to move into town was made. My brothers were enthusiastic about the idea.

"Grouse!" said Bobby. "I'll be able to visit my friends from school."

"Yeah, me too," said Maxie. "We won't have to walk twenty thousand miles to school anymore either."

(Maxie was always prone to exaggeration.)

"We can climb Nan's apple trees," said Kevin.

"Yeah, and we can play in the paddock next

door," said Georgie.

The double block next to Nan and Pop's place was empty and usually covered in long grass.

When the time came to move, my brothers enthusiastically helped Dad with cleaning our yard and packing up. My sister was too young to fully understand but joined in the general atmosphere of flurry and excitement, eagerly trying to help Mum. She obediently tottered out to the verandah with small pieces of rubbish and dropped them on the pile of unwanted items ready to be taken to the rubbish tip. I seemed to be the only one upset about moving. My mother tried to bring me round by highlighting the advantages of the move.

"Just think, you won't have such a long walk to school anymore."

That had no effect at all since I enjoyed the walk to school.

"You can help Nan make scones and cakes."

Even this had no impact on my pig-headed resistance. Mum tried one last time.

"You'll have lots of fun with Nan in the evenings. You know you like listening to her songs and stories."

That one almost weakened my resolve because I, like my brothers, loved sitting at Nan's feet while she stomped out old tunes. She sat outside on a creaky wooden box singing folk songs and sea shanties, accompanying herself on the piano accordion and the mouth organ, and tapped her foot to the beat. Some of those sea shanties were quite bawdy and probably unfit for young ears, but that never stopped Nan. We were too young and probably too innocent to be aware of sexual innuendo; it was the music and the fun atmosphere we enjoyed and her stories were seductively scary.

In the end, I was not persuaded by any of my mother's arguments. Our small rented cottage nestled in the Australian bush had been the only home I knew. I hated the thought of being in town with houses and people everywhere. Stubbornly, I dug my heels in and refused to change my mind.

Despite my opposition the move continued. Dad made frequent trips into town with an assortment of items piled high on the back of the truck. Bobby and Maxie squashed together in the cabin with Dad and helped with the unloading at the other end.

The final day meant hours of hard work for my parents and excitement for my brothers. It was almost dark when the last piece of furniture had been loaded on the back of the truck. The boys had jumped up and spread themselves out among the household items and settled down for the journey to their new home. Mum carried Irene, who was sleeping and wrapped in rugs, out to the truck and settled her on the seat in the cabin.

This was the day I had dreaded, had convinced myself would never really come. At some point in the afternoon I had climbed into the big old apple tree next to the dunny. I climbed as high as I could so that no one would find me.

The truck was ready to go, its motor running. I heard them calling me but I did not respond. After a while they stopped calling. The motor revved loudly. Maxie yelled to me with an urgent tone in his voice. Despite my brothers' consistent tormenting of me they were always quick to protect me when they thought it was necessary. In some quirky way our constant squabbling probably strengthened our sibling bonds. Now, Maxie was afraid that I would be left on my own. It wasn't until the truck started to move that the same fear engulfed me. I shinned down the tree as fast as I could and ran toward the truck.

"She's coming, Dad," Maxie called. The truck slowed and came to a halt as I scrambled into the back with the other kids.

"She's here, Dad," called Maxie, relief evident in his voice. The others joined in so that a chorus of voices announced my arrival.

The truck moved forward once more. I was still

sullen and defiant but I felt that I had at least made a stand. Of course, it was like water off a duck's back to my parents who were by now quite experienced in the ways of children. They knew exactly how to handle me. As far as they were concerned it was just another one of my sulks.

However, perhaps it was more than that. Perhaps in my childhood innocence some intuition told me that the move from the Bonang cottage did, in fact, mark the end of the happiest years in the life of our family.

Chapter 12

SIXTY-NINE-YEAR OLD OLIVE WELCOMED US into her three bedroom weatherboard home in Salisbury Street with open arms. She didn't seem to mind that there were now six children and three adults in the house she and Pop had quietly enjoyed for years. The house trembled under the onslaught of running feet and reverberated with the sounds of children laughing, shouting and crying. That the house was on a big double block was a blessing because it meant, as my mother put it, 'the kids had room to run wild'.

Rose bushes graced the front yard of Nan's place. In one corner stood a loquat tree whose dense canopy and abundant succulent yellow fruit attested to its age and fertility. A cement path led visitors from the gate to the front door via large semi-circular stone steps, caressed on both sides by the pink and blue blooms of rotund hydrangea bushes. These bushes were perfect places for us kids to hide whenever we 'ran away from home'. The front veranda was where

Nan and Pop had often sat together on warm evenings to watch 'the passing parade' and wave at old
Bernie Johnson across the road pottering around in
his vegetable garden.

My brothers quickly discovered that it was possible to run from one end of Nan's house to the other
along the wide hallway. They delighted in the opportunity to charge through the back door, straight
along the hall, out through the front door using the
hall rug as a slide for the last section, then around the
side path to appear at the back door again for a
repeat performance, always competing to see who
could do it in the fastest time. On one occasion, the
neighbour's pony, either inspired by the boys or
frightened by something, actually galloped through
the back door and along the hall out to the front
veranda.

The back part of the house consisted of a wash
house, with a copper heated on wash days by a wood
fire beneath it. The outside back door separated this
laundry section from the kitchen; the hub of the
house from which tantalizing aromas beckoned us
and where freshly baked scones, cakes and pies often
covered the table.

Like her mahogany dining table, Nan's wood
cupboard was a source of enchantment for us. It was
next to the stove in the kitchen and could be accessed

from inside as well as outside. We could enter the cupboard through the door on the kitchen side, clamber over the pile of wood then depart, like elves, through the small door which was used for placing the wood into the cupboard from the outside. The seductive charm of Nan's house and Nan herself eventually stopped me brooding over the loss of our Bonang home even though I missed the bush: its earthy smell, the silence of isolation, the wide open spaces and especially the songs of the birds.

Dad rose early on the first morning in our new home to take the truck out to the bush to collect a load of firewood. Instead of the heavy work of cutting sleepers he had become a 'wood merchant' or so it said on the driver's side door of our old green Commer truck. He planned to keep a stack of sawn logs in the back yard ready for delivery. The boys were going with him, eagerly dragging themselves from their beds despite their hard work of the day before.

Mum and Nan were in the kitchen early, stoking the fire in the wood stove and getting the kettle on the boil.

"You look after the little ones, Myrtle," Nan said with a smile. "And I'll look after the grown-ups."

Mum prepared five bowls of Weet-bix; one for each of my brothers and one for me. Irene was still asleep in her cot and would be fed later.

"We don't have any red coals for toasting bread, I'm afraid," Nan said when my father entered the kitchen. "I've not long lit the fire."

"Never mind," said Dad. He strode to the bench and began slicing a loaf of bread with the large carving knife. "Just cook it on the top of the stove. That'll do me."

He handed two thick slices of the white bread to Olive who placed them on the blackened cast iron hot plate of the stove. On another hot plate, a frypan sizzled with lamb chops, sausages and eggs. Nan shuffled the food around in the frypan with an egg lifter and, with the fingers of her free hand, she turned the bread over from time to time.

"Stop that, you two." Bobby attempted an air of authority in his tone as he chastised the twins who were fighting over the jug of milk. This was the milk from Nan's pet cow.

"Mum, the babies are slopping milk all over Nan's table," he added.

Dad sat down at the head of the table. Mum placed a cup of tea in front of him. A plate of fried food that Nan had transferred from the pan followed.

Georgie released his grasp on the milk jug and turned to glare at Bobby.

"We're not babies," he said firmly. "We're big now. We're seven."

Nan placed Dad's two slices of toast on his plate. Kevin had also lost interest in the milk jug and joined his twin in his protest.

"Mu…um. Tell Bobby to stop calling us babies."

"Yeah," said Georgie. "Tell him, Mum. Irene's the baby."

The twins had been called 'the babies' since the day they were born. Bobby, now aware of his father's presence, refrained from arguing further but hissed at them under his breath. "Babies!"

Mum was mindful of Nan, afraid the noise would irritate her.

"That'll be enough from you lot," she said.

She looked across at Dad. His head was bent over the plate as he used his teeth to expertly skin the last of the cooked meat from a chop bone.

"Dad," she said.

He raised his eyes to look at her and nodded. They always seemed to understand each other's glances. He placed the bone back on his plate and picked up the second piece of toast.

"Right, you boys," he said. "Off you go and wait in the truck."

Immediately, their argument was forgotten. All four of them pushed their chairs back from the table and headed for the door, each jostling to be first to race out to the back yard and climb into the truck. Dad laughed as he watched them disappear. He finished his toast, gulped down the last of his tea and stood up. Mum handed him a thermos of tea and the lunch box she had prepared earlier containing sandwiches and apples.

"Wait a minute, Myrtle," said Nan, reaching for a large cake tin in the cupboard. "Pop these scones in. I made them yesterday."

She wrapped a half a dozen brown-topped scones in a clean tea towel and handed them to Mum.

"Thanks, Mum." My mother placed the scones into the box before releasing it to Dad's grasp.

"Well, I'm off for another day of hard yakka," said my father with a grin.

He tucked the box under his arm and hurried out the door. I heard the truck engine spluttering into life. Then the rumbling of the truck along the back driveway announced the departure of my father and brothers. The house seemed strangely quiet.

"What about you, Myrtle?" asked Nan, frypan in one hand and egglifter in the other. "What will you have for breakfast?"

My mother laughed. "You sit down and have your own breakfast, Mum. I can look after myself."

"Not on your first day in your new home," said

Nan as she placed the frypan back on top of the stove. "You sit down and I'll cook you something."

Mum laughed and sat down.

"Careful," she said to Nan, "I could get used to this."

Nan smiled and picked up two pink sausages from the pile on a tray on the bench.

"Sausages?" she said displaying the conjoined casings of ground meat.

"Thanks, Mum. One will do. I usually just have tea and toast with Vegemite."

Because it was expensive, my mother always gave first priority for meat to Dad and us. The accepted wisdom of the time was that men needed meat because of the hard work they did and children needed it because they were growing.

At breakfast time it was usually only Dad who had meat. The rest of us had just the one cooked meal on most days although Mum would often include cold meat or leftovers in the sandwiches she made for our lunch.

"Well, today you're having an egg as well," said Nan. "It'll do us both good: sausages and eggs."

So that was how Nan welcomed Mum to her new home. My mother's years of living in the bush were over but not her years of living with ghosts.

Chapter 13

SLEEPING QUARTERS IN OUR NEW house were only slightly less cramped than in the Bonang house. I shared my grandmother's bedroom although I did not think of it as a room I shared. It was my grandmother's room and I laid no claim to it in any way other than the place where I slept. My four brothers slept in the small room across the hall from the front parlour which was now a bedroom for my parents and Irene, whose cot nestled in a corner.

At first, the boys seemed to be constantly running through the house. Scolding them barely diminished their enthusiasm for this activity. In the end, Mum gave them permission to play in the vacant lot next door. They grasped this new adventure with gusto, playing Cowboys and Indians, stalking each other in the tall grass amid yells and whoops that could probably be heard for miles around.

My mother seemed to welcome our boisterousness. I think she viewed it as evidence her kids were happy and healthy. However, she was fearful that our wild behaviour and noisy exuberance, fully developed from years of living in the open spaces of the bush, would not be appreciated by Nan's neighbours. Nan dismissed Mum's worries with a wave of her hand.

"They're just doing what children should do," she said. "The neighbours'll get used to them."

My mother laughed.

"What about you, Mum?" she asked. "Will you get used to them?"

"The kids make me feel young," Nan said. "It's good to have young ones around the house."

Nan went back to puffing contentedly on her pipe. It had been Pop's pipe. She had taken it over after his death even though she had not previously been a smoker. Nan's impish grin answered Mum's bemused expression the first time she saw her mother-in-law smoking Pop's pipe.

"Kinda keeps him with me," Nan said.

The feel of his pipe, the intimacy of it and of course the familiar aroma of the tobacco must have given her the experience of Pop, almost as though he were still alive. Having us around must have also provided a suitable distraction from her grief because she adjusted well to the unaccustomed explosion of children in her house. One concern she did have at first was that Bloomers, her pet cow, might be frightened with so many noisy children around. But the cow did not seem to care at all.

Bloomers had been with Nan and Pop on the dairy farm and when they moved into town the cow moved with them. Nan kept Bloomers in the back yard which was not fenced off. In the mornings, Bloomers was usually tied up to the clothes line. It was probably not the wisest choice of stakes because Bloomers got her name from her habit of eating almost anything, including a pair of Nan's large bloomers from the line. In the afternoons Nan untied Bloomers so she could wander off to the vacant block next door to eat some of the delicious green grass.

"Don't go beyond that paddock. You hear me?" Nan would call out as the cow dawdled away with a flick of her tail.

Bloomers was an obedient cow but she did once get Nan into a spot of bother. One morning there was a knock on Nan's front door. This was unusual because most people would walk along the side path, past the kitchen window and around to the back door. The front door was only for strangers and bad news. That's what it was this particular morning: bad news. When Nan opened the door, old Bernie Johnson was standing there with a thunderous look on his face. Old Bernie lived across from Nan and down a few doors. He didn't care too much for people. He didn't really care too much for anything except his garden, especially his dahlias which had won prizes at the Bairnsdale flower show.

When Nan opened the door, old Bernie said, "Mrs Rowley, your damn cow's eating my dahlias."

Nan sprang into action! "That stupid cow," she said.

She was off down the front steps in her slippers and virtually rolled down the path with her walking stick propelling her along.

"If I've told her once, I've told her a thousand times; don't go beyond that paddock," she muttered to herself.

Off she went across the road and down to Bernie's place. Sure enough, there was the 'damn cow' happily munching away, the wine-red petals of Bernie's prize dahlia's still hanging from the corner of her mouth.

Nan waved her walking stick and shouted. The poor cow got such a fright it bolted. Nan went after her. Past the rows of dahlias, through Bernie Johnson's cauliflower patch and out through the gate. Across the road, down the hill and around the block they went, both of them kicking up dust.

It was when they were coming back up the hill behind Nan's place that Nan gave up the chase. The cow kept going.

Nan hobbled down the well-worn dirt path in the back yard, huffing and puffing and muttering and shaking her head. She was a bit taken aback when she saw Bloomers still tethered to the clothes line happily munching on the grass around the base of the post. It never occurred to Nan that the cow in old Bernie's dahlia patch wasn't Bloomers. She hadn't stopped to think that it was morning and Bloomers was only untethered in the afternoons.

Nan pulled up abreast of Bloomers and took a moment to catch her breath.

"You stupid cow," she said as she moved on towards the back door.

Some might have called Nan eccentric but she was the only Nan I had in my life and I thought she was the best Nan ever. She took pleasure in teaching me how to make cakes, pastry and scones.

"Anyone can cook meat and vegetables. But baking? Now that's an art," she said.

On Saturday afternoons the two of us would have fun together in the kitchen. I learned to make cakes and sponges long before I could boil an egg. Her favourite things to make were scones; we made those a lot.

"Making good scones is a skill not many people learn," Nan said. "I'll teach you how to do it. First you need a good recipe. Get me that recipe book in the top drawer."

Her CWA recipe book was in constant use. The CWA (Country Women's Association) is an organisation that supports women living in isolated areas. The cakes and scones made by their members and often sold at fund raising street stalls were legendary. Many of these recipes were collected and published. Most country women had a copy of at least one CWA recipe book.

I opened Nan's up to the page for scones which was yellow from a blend of milk, egg and flour stains. She had her bowl ready on the table with the ingredients arranged around it: flour, salt, butter, bicarbonate of soda, cream of tartar and milk.

"Now," she said. "Read out to me what it says."

"Sift flour and salt. Lightly rub in the butter. Then sift in the raising agents and mix well."

"That's right," said Nan.

However, she demonstrated a blithe disregard for the precise instructions of the CWA experts, throwing all the dry ingredients into the bowl and mixing them together with her hands. Then she poured the milk in and stirred the mixture roughly with a wooden spoon.

"Now what does it say, little'un?"

"Add all the milk and mix lightly to a spongy

dough."

"I've already done that step," said Nan.

"Knead very lightly and roll out to half an inch thick."

Nan lifted the mixture onto the floured table and flattened it with her hand.

"Cut out with a two inch cutter."

Nan grabbed a bone-handled knife and cut the flattened dough into squares.

"Brush with egg or milk."

Nan splashed water over the tops of her lumpy squares.

"Bake in a hot oven."

"That bit is important," she said.

She sprinkled some flour on a baking tray and placed it in the oven for a few seconds. When it turned brown, she nodded her head in approval. Using a tea-towel to protect her hands, she removed the baking tray. Then she sprinkled more flour on the baking tray and together we lined up her rough scone squares on it. Into the oven they went. Ten minutes later, out they came, browned on the top, three times as big as they were when they went in and each one as light as a feather.

"Perfect," she said. "It helps to have a good recipe."

In the summer evenings Nan encouraged our

noisy ebullience with sing-alongs. She taught us the words to the songs so that we could sing with her. Since none of us seemed to have inherited our father and grandmother's keen ear for a tune, the result probably sounded like a raucous cacophony of strangled canaries. In our blissful ignorance we belted out the tunes together, rising to a crackling crescendo during choruses such as: *Hooray and up she rises, earlie in the morning.* We also performed a rousing rendition of a song called *Deep in the Heart of Texas.* We clapped our hands with the tune and my brothers hollered like cowboys at regular intervals.

Dad would sometimes join in the singing sessions but often, tired after his day's work, he preferred to sit in Pop's chair reading the paper.

Less than a year after we moved into our new home, Mum was expecting another child. Dad had joked that with Irene, now three years old, sleeping in their room they would have little opportunity for 'hanky panky' as she grew older. He told Mum they should 'make hay while the sun shines'. That had made my mother blush but apparently they had done just as he suggested. Peter, Mum and Dad's seventh child, was born in May 1960.

"Look at that," Dad said proudly when he first laid eyes on the newborn. "Another chip off the old block, eh, Mum?"

My mother might have been subdued in her response because she had lost a lot of blood and was suffering from anaemia. The doctor warned her against having more children. However, my father was always in high spirits on the birth of a new child and Peter's birth was no exception. He held the baby, cocooned in soft rugs, high above his head to show him off to the rest of us.

"Look at him. You couldn't wish for a healthier baby," he grinned. As Peter's tiny fingers grasped his, he added, "and strong as a Mallee bull like his dad. Comes from good stock, he does."

I am sure the arrival of Peter gave my parents hope. Dad's poor health must have weighed heavily on their minds. They might have reasoned that there could be nothing seriously wrong with Dad if he was able to produce a strong, healthy child.

As time passed, Dad's tiredness became worse and the strenuous physical labour of work in the bush eventually proved too much for him despite his determined efforts to continue. Peter had not long passed his second birthday when Dad had to give up being a wood merchant. He started working as a yardman at Marshall's hotel, known to the locals as 'the top pub' because it was at the top end of the main street. There another hotel at the bottom end of the main street which was, of course, 'the bottom pub'.

I am not sure that a diagnosis had been made at this stage because I never heard either of my parents mention the name of my father's illness. With my ability to make myself into an invisible listener, I feel I would have discovered this secret if they had known it. On the other hand, it is possible they had by this stage been informed that it was myeloid leukaemia but did not want to say the words aloud.

It must have seemed incomprehensible to Mum that a young man, after all Dad had not yet reached forty when the symptoms first appeared, so physically strong and positive and passionate about life could suddenly have that life threatened by a serious illness.

I think my father faced the possibility that he would succumb to the disease before Mum did. I am sure that each time he went to the Alfred Hospital for further tests, now often accompanied by Nan, Mum imagined they would find a cure. She probably envisaged him running through the door on his return with jubilation beaming from every fibre in his body. The nightmare would be over and she could smile and say, "See, I knew you would get better." Instead, he seemed to become weaker.

He had started to talk about making preparations 'in case anything happens to me'. They went through the paperwork together and wrote to the appropriate government agencies to ensure Mum had all the necessary documents to claim the widow's pension.

"We'll always have a roof over our heads, that's the most important thing," Mum said.

Dad nodded. "But you'll have a lot of mouths to feed too, Myrtle. You'll need money for that and for their education."

"That's what the Child Endowment is for," she told him with a smile. "With that and the widow's pension we'll be just fine. Not that I intend being a widow any time soon, mind."

She laughed but his serious face sobered her mood.

"Honestly, Dad. We'll be all right," she said. "Bobby is already doing part time work and Maxie will do the same. They'll both be working full time soon and June is smart enough to get a scholarship. As far as food is concerned, well, we don't buy that much anyway, what with all the food everyone gives us."

People in the community were aware of Dad's illness and wanted to help. The local shopkeepers knew him well. There was always something given to Mum every time she went up to the street. The baker gave her bread he said he could not sell. The grocer gave her the biscuits that had become broken in the tins and could not be sold. The market gardener gave her boxes of fruit and vegetables. Often she simply found boxes of food that had been left at the back door by individual townspeople.

"Don't worry," Mum told him. "You have so many friends in this town your family is not likely to go without if anything happens to you."

He sighed. There was so much in that sigh; his regret, his loss and his grief.

Looking back, I know I missed much of their story simply because I was absorbed in my own world, but their love for each other was always evident.

I can imagine them that night in the warmth of their bed as they lay quietly together. Across the room, Irene and Peter lay sleeping in the cot Irene had once had to herself. In that silence, in the darkness of their bedroom, Mum might have finally accepted the cruel reality that her husband, the man who had loved and protected her year after year with the deepest passion and the purest commitment, was sick enough to die. I imagine the tears rolling down her cheeks. I see her hand reaching for his under the covers and squeezing it. I see his fingers closing over hers.

Chapter 14

ALL THIS TIME, AND FOR many more years, we (the Rowley children) were completely unaware of the Bishop children; our three half-siblings who were living out their lives without their mother.

At the age of three and a half, Myrtle's first child Bertie was placed in a Home temporarily when the marriage of Myrtle and Henry Bishop fell apart in 1942. In those days the NSW Child Welfare Department issued licences to 'respectable' women who wished to set up a Children's Home. A woman who needed to find a way to survive without a husband, such as a widow or deserted wife, was able to make a living by converting her house to a Children's Home. No qualifications were required, no training was necessary. Children might be placed in such a Home permanently or for a period of time during a family crisis. It seems likely that Bertie, Audrey and Noel were placed temporarily in a Home of this kind.

Unlike his sister and brother, Bertie was taken out

of care after a short time. He went to live with his paternal grandmother and grandfather at 536 David Street, Albury, where he stayed until he was around nine years old. Why were the other two children left in institutions? Perhaps there were financial reasons but I believe the main reason was that Agnes Bishop had got it into her head that Audrey and Noel were not her son's children. This woman's spitefulness came through strongly during my research into what happened to my mother. I have no doubt that Agnes was the instigator behind the rumours and events that led to Myrtle's three children being taken from her.

Society made it easy for Agnes Bishop's malevolence to bear fruit. At that time a woman could be declared an unfit mother, which would result in her children being removed from her care, simply because the children had been absent from school on several occasions. It was also a time when a neighbour or a relative, such as a child's grandmother could, and often did, cause children to be placed in Homes even when the children were living in safe, secure and suitable family situations. Such an incident is related in Joanna Penglase's book *Orphans of the Living*: Sylvia Baker's maternal grandmother who 'had never thought our father was good enough for her daughter' asked the NSW Department to investigate how the children were being cared for after the children's mother died. This resulted in Sylvia and her siblings being placed in a Home despite, or because of, the fact that the children's father was willingly caring for his children with the help of a housekeeper.

Bertie was not able to give me detailed information about his life with his grandparents, but I imagine he spent his childhood engaged in activities common to other children living in Albury at the time: picking mushrooms and blackberries, making 'flying saucers' out of dry cowpats, letting off firecrackers and indulging in other harmless mischief. He might have made a billycart out of a wooden fruit box from the grocer and raced it down a hill with other children. Perhaps his grandmother allowed him to go to the pictures when there was a Saturday matinee on at the local cinema.

His grandparents cared for Bertie and looked after him. However, during his time with them, Bertie's grandmother took the opportunity to poison his mind about his mother, telling him Myrtle was a slut and a bitch, among other things. This makes me very angry not just on my mother's behalf but because of how it must have made Bertie feel to believe his mother was such a person and to grow up thinking she had callously abandoned him.

Bertie recalled that as a young child he was once approached by a woman at the gate of the house in David Street. She alighted from a bicycle to hand him a gift of toys but he was quickly snatched away from her by his grandmother.

"You mustn't go near that woman. She'll steal you away," Agnes Bishop told him.

The memory of this incident stayed with Bertie because he wondered if the woman offering the gift was his mother. From the description that he gave me when I met him, I believe it was. If this was Myrtle, her actions do not seem consistent with a mother who 'deserted' her children which was what Henry Bishop claimed. I also think the remark by Bertie's paternal grandmother is revealing. She may have said it merely to frighten the child but her words could also suggest she thought that Myrtle might try to get her children back, which throws further doubt on the desertion accusation.

Technically, perhaps Myrtle could be described as deserting her children for if she was being forced to take them on as a single parent she simply could not have done so. As a woman on her own in the 1940s and the daughter of a widow, Myrtle would not have stood a chance of being able to support herself and her children. She would not have been eligible to claim social security payments and work would not have been an option. Given the prejudices toward married women and/or mothers in the workforce at that time she would have found it almost impossible to get a job. With no kindergartens, child care centres or 'before and after' school care, she would also have had to find someone to take care of the children while she was at work. Myrtle would have found it as difficult as Joanna Penglase's mother who was forced to place her daughters 'in care' in the 1940s. In *Orphans of the Living*, Joanna writes:

'What else could my mother do? In the immediate post war era there was an acute housing shortage and very little government or community assistance. Women's wages were low and not equal to a male – a breadwinner's – wage. But how could my mother go to work, if she had found a job? Who would look after her children, one of them a baby? Even finding accommodation was difficult. She lived in a much stricter, more judgemental, moral environment than we do now, and women on their own – especially with children – were suspect.' Joanna Penglase could just as easily be talking about my mother.

I wonder if Myrtle allowed herself to be named a deserter, or perhaps was pressured to allow it, because that was the preferable option that would be acceptable grounds for divorce. The other options were adultery and cruelty, both of which would have resulted in significant newspaper coverage which, especially in a relatively small place like Albury, would have done a great deal of harm to the family's reputation. This choice would also have made the children the targets of gossiping tongues.

Perhaps Myrtle felt that she *had* virtually deserted her children because she had lost her will to care in the normal way as a result of post natal depression. People who were placed in Homes as children often mention they were put there as a result of their mother suffering a 'nervous breakdown' after the birth of a child. Such conditions were not discussed and often not considered worthy of medical treatment. In Myrtle's case it might not have even been post-natal depression but simply depression as a result of spending over four years with an uncaring husband while enduring the manipulative influence of a mother-in-law who did not want her around. However, rather than desert her children, Myrtle appears to have made every effort to remain close to them until she eventually had to face the heartbreaking reality of her circumstances.

From my knowledge of her as a mother I know that she would never willingly give up her children. Mum was a totally committed mother who went out of her way to make our young lives fun, interesting, healthy and educational. She spent time and thought on the things she could do with us, and for us, such as making an Easter egg trail so that we would have fun following the route and finding eggs hidden in unlikely places – a few small chocolate eggs but mostly painted boiled hen's eggs. It didn't matter what sort of eggs, Mum understood that it was the fun of searching and discovering that gave us joy. I know she would have given the same commitment to her first three children had circumstances been different. Perhaps her unceasing dedication to us was partly because of shame that she had had to relinquish her other children but if that is the case it only reinforces my opinion that she cared about them.

When I first began my research I, in my ignorance, could not understand why she had not fought tooth and nail to keep her children with her. I am now in a better position to understand the complex issues involved. Sometimes I berate myself for having had such unkind thoughts and being so quick to pass judgement. There could have been several reasons why Myrtle did not, or could not, fight to keep her children. For one thing, she did not have the financial resources to take care of them. Added to that was the likelihood that she was bereft of the emotional resources to fight for them and because of that possibly felt they would be better off with their father or in a Home.

It was not Myrtle but the children's father who placed them in orphanages. Henry Bishop claimed, I assume in order to justify his actions, that Myrtle said she couldn't look after the children. We don't know for sure that Myrtle said that. After all, the statement comes from a man who did his very best to avoid his responsibility to his children and was only too ready to believe his mother's malicious lies about his wife. However, if Myrtle did say it there could be many reasons why. Perhaps she meant she could not do it on her own and needed help. I also wonder if Henry Bishop told her she would receive no financial assistance from him. Since he believed at least two of the children were not his, he would have felt justified in withdrawing his financial support.

Admittedly, in those days it would have been difficult for a single father to rear three children. Putting children in an orphanage or Home was not only a common solution to family breakdown but seen as appropriate and best for the children. Therefore, I must (grudgingly) allow that purely practical reasons might have been behind Henry Bishop's decision to place his children in Homes. Whatever the reason, Audrey and Noel remained in institutions after Bertie went to live with his grandparents.

At around the age of nine, Bertie became too wild for his grandmother to handle. The situation was apparently brought to a head when Bertie found some detonator caps in the glove box of an unlocked car. Not knowing what they were, but intrigued by them, he placed the caps in his pocket and continued on his way, which happened to be along the railway line. Perhaps still thinking about his new 'toys', he did not hear the train coming until it was almost too late. Bertie scuttled out of the way in time but the train driver reported the incident to the police. No doubt the train driver considered a young boy wandering along the railway tracks to be a tragedy waiting to happen. Had he also known about the detonator caps he would surely have been horrified. The Albury police, when they interviewed Bertie, *were* horrified and took the matter seriously. Bertie's father, probably in response to a summons from Agnes Bishop, travelled from Queensland to Albury to sort out the problem.

The aftermath of this incident which resulted in court proceedings was that the family decided it was time for Bertie's father to take charge of his eldest son. Consequently, Bertie travelled with Henry Bishop by train to Manly, Queensland 1500 kilometres away to join his step-mother and three half-siblings. A two-day journey on a steam train might have been a dream come true for a young boy but it was extremely unpleasant for nine-year-old Bertie who suffered with motion sickness the whole way.

In his new home, Bertie experienced some initial adjustment difficulties. Agnes Bishop, who did not approve of her son's second wife any more than she had approved of Myrtle, had given Bertie a mission. He was to cause as much trouble as he could in his new home with the aim of breaking up his father's marriage. Clearly, no woman was good enough for Agnes Bishop's son.

Bertie was essentially an obedient child and did his best to carry out his grandmother's wishes. He became so troublesome that he was sent for a period of time to Boys Town: a boys' residential facility and school established by the De La Salle Brothers. In recent years, former residents have spoken of sexual and physical abuse they suffered in this facility. Boys Town was one of 150 orphanages and detention centres in Queensland under review by the Forde Inquiry which 'encompassed the period from 1911 to 1999'. The Inquiry 'found significant evidence of abuse and neglect of children' which 'included emotional, physical, sexual and systems abuse'. Bertie did not speak to me of his experience at Boys Town so I do not know if he was an abuse victim during his time there.

He was eventually returned to the family home where his step-mother did her best to look after him and include him in the family. He enjoyed spending time with his father, especially helping him tinker with cars. However, his previous behaviour had impacted on their relationship and they did not establish a close bond.

During the time Bertie lived in Albury with his grandparents, he was never taken to visit his sister, Audrey, who was less than ten kilometres away at St John's Orphanage in Thurgoona, then considered to be on the outskirts of Albury but now a suburb.

Chapter 15

"IF YOU WANT TO KNOW what it was like in the Orphanage, read *Orphanage Survivors: A true story of St. John's, Thurgoona*, by Howard C. Jones," Audrey said when I asked her about her childhood at St John's.

Because she was not able to remember her life there in detail, I did as she suggested and bought a copy of the book. Audrey told me that she was in one of the group photos reprinted in *Orphanage Survivors* so I decided to see if I could pick her out. Having listened to her talk about some of her experiences, her feelings about the Orphanage and how she saw herself as a 'throw-away child', I looked for a little girl who might have that reflected in her face. It did not take me long to pick her out and Audrey later verified that I was correct. I also read about many of the girls who were in St John's; an institution which was founded by the Sisters of Mercy in 1882 and created in the 'strict discipline of the Irish Catholic orphanage'. Some of the women have fond memories of their girlhood in the Orphanage but Audrey and others have painful memories.

Marie Rooney who arrived at St John's with her three sisters in 1952 states: 'I was nine. The four of us huddled together at the big front gate and cried for a week. We were waiting for our family to come and get us but no one came. It was frightening.'

I also heard the poignant phrase 'no-one came' from Audrey's lips.

The Rooney sisters eventually settled in and Marie recalls: 'It was a tough life, because there was no one to cuddle you when you felt bad, but eventually there were lots of good times.'

For Ruth Robinson, 'It was always bad. We went without meals for punishment, or were locked up or stretched across a bed and flogged.'

I read about Margaret Coyne who 'was a very naughty girl'.

'The nuns used to put her in the cellar and put a hessian bag on her for a dress. Once they put her in a big flour bin. I was there when they tied her to a tree by an anthill,' recalls Olive Bryan.

Virginia Savige stated: 'We didn't keep anything. I remember being given a doll in a big box, but it was taken away.'

One woman recalls that on her first night at the Orphanage she refused to eat the sago she was given so a nun 'grabbed her by the hair and force-fed her'.

'When I proceeded to spew, she just kept spooning it up and feeding it to me until the superior made her stop.'

Having several acres of land allowed the Orphanage to grow most of their own food and keep cows on the property. The staff and older girls made butter and bread and most of the girls worked in the vegetable garden. They also rose very early in the morning to milk the cows and separate the milk.

'I was nine years old and we went barefoot,' recalls Ruth Robinson. 'When it was cold we waited for the cow to drop her shit and we put our foot in it to warm it up.'

The girls at St John's lived in daily fear of punishment. One girl recalls being belted and ordered to stand in the dark until 2 a.m. because she had asked if she could put her cardigan on. Perceived bad behaviour or sins such as bedwetting would result in girls being deprived of food, flogged or locked in cupboards. This sort of physical and emotional cruelty was not uncommon. Neither was it uncommon for an orphanage to use a small, confined space such as the cupboard under the stairs to lock children in. A child could be kept in isolation for hours, or even days.

Audrey recalls these severe punishments and remembers spending hours scrubbing the floor area of the Orphanage verandas with a small brush – another common penance. She was in trouble a lot and was often punished for things she did not do. On one occasion, Audrey had to kneel on the hard floor with her hands held out while a nun repeatedly slapped her palms with a cane. One nun vented her anger on Audrey by repeatedly whipping the backs of her legs with a cane, determined to make the child cry.

"I'll break you if it's the last thing I do!" yelled the nun.

However, Audrey refused to cry. When the beating was over, she told the nun she had been punished for something she did not do.

"You'll be the death of me, yet," retorted the nun.

One day, not long after she arrived at St. John's, probably at the age of three, the nuns dressed Audrey in a pretty blue dress for a visit to her mother. When she returned to the Orphanage after her visit with Myrtle, the nuns yanked the dress off so roughly that her arm was pulled out of its socket. She curled up on her bed and cried. Later, she was pacified with a bar of chocolate which must have been a luxury for any orphanage child.

The Orphanage environment was a harsh one and, like the other inmates, Audrey was not shown any affection. She yearned for love and she yearned to be touched; touched in the casual, familiar way that happens as a matter of course in a family situation.

A typical day was an early rise in the morning for a 6 a.m. shower with the other 50 or 60 inmates. Their naked bodies were exposed to the watchful eyes of the nuns standing guard, fully dressed in their habits. Before eating their breakfast of lumpy porridge, toast and milky tea, the girls were required to say prayers. After breakfast they were shepherded to the school room for the day's lessons.

No food was offered at the 11 a.m. break but at lunch time the girls filed into the dining hall for stew and bread before returning to the class room. After school, the girls had to work; setting the table for dinner, washing dirty dishes and scrubbing in the laundry. The sound of a cow bell signalled dinner time. The evening meal was usually the same as lunch with an added treat such as fruit and custard. School homework had to be completed before bedtime at around 7 p.m. At weekends, there was time for play provided the girls did not participate in unladylike activities such as climbing trees for which they would be severely punished.

There were few acts of kindness but on one occasion Audrey, a frail and skinny child, was peering longingly through the kitchen window at the women who were baking and preparing food when one of the older women gave her two slices of bread with jam and cream. It was a rare treat that she remembers to this day.

She also recalls visits from her mother. Later, Etti Webb (Myrtle's mother) visited her. I suspect Etti visited when Myrtle was no longer able to because she had left Albury to start her new life in Orbost. However, as time passed, Audrey recalls that 'no one came'.

Perhaps Etti Webb felt unable to continue the visits for personal reasons. It is also possible that her visits ceased because the nuns at the Orphanage thought it would be kinder to Audrey if family members did not visit. This was certainly the case at other orphanages.

Lorraine Davis who was in Launceston Children's Home from the age of three is quoted in *Orphans of the Living* as saying: 'My mother wasn't allowed to visit us at the home, as they thought it would upset us too much.'

Frank Golding, who was in Ballarat Orphanage in the 1940s, relates in his submission to the *2004 Australian Senate Inquiry* into children in institutional care how the superintendent claimed: 'Your father upsets you; I'm going to cut out these visits.'

I have no proof that Etti ceased her visits as a result of advice from the Orphanage; there might have been an entirely different reason. Another possible reason is that once the final legal documents sealed Henry Bishop's custody of the children in 1947, he exercised his power and desire for revenge by forbidding Myrtle and her mother to visit. I have no proof of that either.

Like most children in orphanages, Audrey fantasised about having a family. She spent her young years wanting desperately to be someone's daughter. At about the same time that Myrtle gave birth to my twin brothers Kevin and Georgie in 1952, Audrey's dream of being part of a family almost came true. A Catholic couple applied to adopt the lonely twelve-year-old. Permission had to be given by Audrey's father who had retained legal custody of Audrey and her brother, Noel.

Unfortunately, Henry Bishop, who was Church of England, refused to allow the adoption to go ahead on the basis that he did not wish his daughter to become a Catholic. This is mystifying since the children at St John's were brought up as Catholics anyway. All Audrey wanted was a family. She wanted to be hugged and kissed goodnight.

She did not know whether her mother was still alive. Furthermore, she did not know she had an older brother living a few kilometres from St John's and a younger brother 400 kilometres away, across the state border in Ballarat, Victoria.

Chapter 16

BALLARAT, JUST OVER ONE HUNDRED kilometres from Melbourne, is home to the Wathaurong people and was first settled by Europeans in 1837. In less than twenty years the region developed dramatically into a city of 100 000 people as a result of the 1851 Gold Rush. The city's affluence led to an increase in public buildings such as the Ballarat District Orphan Asylum in Victoria Street which was built on an old mining ground. This large two storey red brick mansion of Gothic design accommodating 200 children was built in the 1860s.

By 1945 when Noel, the youngest of Myrtle's first three children, was sent there, the institution had been renamed Ballarat Orphanage. It was set on several acres and included a swimming pool, a library, a football ground and tennis courts.

In those days, there was no attempt to keep siblings together in orphanages. In his submission to the Senate Inquiry, Frank Golding writes: 'The staff saw no reason to treat brothers and sisters as part of a family. Instead, children were separated into age groups and some siblings were even sent to different orphanages.'

Boys in the Riverina district were usually sent to Gumleigh Boys Home 180 kilometres from Albury in Wagga Wagga. I do not know why Noel was sent instead to a city 400 kilometres away in a different state. It is possible Gumleigh did not take toddlers; Noel was three years old at the time of his placement. It could have been that there were simply no vacancies. The abundance of children in Australia as a result of the post war baby boom meant there were not enough places for children in the available Homes.

Arriving at an orphanage must have been an especially traumatic time for children who were sometimes taken by their parents, sometimes sent by train with a relative and sometimes escorted by the police. Phyllis Davies was sent on her own, at the age of nine, from Melbourne to Albury by train. She arrived around midnight after what would probably have been a four or five hour journey in those days. She was to be admitted to St John's Orphanage and was told to 'find a policeman' when she arrived and tell him 'there was a note in my bag'. (*Orphanage Survivors*)

Noel was accompanied by his father on his train journey from Albury to Ballarat Orphanage. He remembers sitting on a park bench at the railway station under a huge flagpole, swinging his feet which were not able to reach the ground. When the train reached Melbourne, Noel and his father took another train to Ballarat. Noel does not recall arriving at the Orphanage but Frank Golding who was there at the same time as Noel, recalled his own arrival vividly in his submission to the Senate Inquiry:

'It was a terrifying experience to be dragged to the doorway of this huge, two-storeyed institution, 'Orphan Asylum' in large letters outside and 200 other orphans inside. I remember it was my brother Bob's fourth birthday so I must have been two and a half. Bill, our half-brother, was a little older.

I snatched at each shaft of the iron fence as the policeman pulled us towards the great double gate. The gravel crunched under our feet as we drew near the dark-red building. Looking up to the balcony on the second floor, Billy read to us the cast iron words 'ORPHAN ASYLUM 1865'. This was a grim place, this Ballarat Orphanage. Solid, like a fortress.

Billy and Bobby clutched my hands tightly as we came to the grand front doors. A child cried down the long passage. Bobby tried to pull back and we joined in. That was futile. Our escort pushed us past the large front doors into the vast entrance hallway where Miss Sharp awaited. Arms crossed, she filled the hallway like a giant. A watch hung from a heavy chain on her massive bosom. She searched our faces. Her scrutiny hurt and my eyes welled up. I whimpered like a timid dog.'

Frank Golding also wrote a book about his childhood called *An Orphan's Escape*, in which he recalls the Orphanage as a grim place with stern staff where 'there was no privacy; not even for the most personal needs'.

Orphanage children slept in dormitories where there was not only a lack of privacy but also no personal space at night. They lived regimented lives under the control and in the presence of authority. An optimistic assessment of Ballarat Orphanage published in the Melbourne newspaper *The Argus* in 1924 states: '...in the little locker assigned to each inmate there is a little store of week-day and Sunday clothing, orderly as in a soldier's kit. And the little people do all this for themselves; the nurse or attendant directs, and nothing more.'

During the day, there was nowhere for children to go to be by themselves. Neither Audrey nor Noel had the luxury that I had of being able to escape from my brothers and the outside world by curling up in the hayshed with a book.

Bath time was another occasion when children in private homes might be afforded some privacy but not orphanage children who had to line up naked and wait their turn. Bath night in orphanages was usually only once a week and, as in many private homes at that time, the bath water would not be changed until all the children had had their baths. Noel remembers sharing the bath with twenty other children on Friday nights when he was in the toddlers' block. They were dried off by the older Orphanage girls in an assembly line.

When they were in their pyjamas, a female staff member read them all a bed-time story. I am glad that Noel at least has this memory of warm interaction with an adult. Such moments were few, and a close relationship with a trusted adult was non-existent. Noel had the same problems as Frank Golding who had no-one to answer the questions that 'gnawed' at his brain. "Where could you turn for answers or reassurance? We dealt with the mysteries and meanings of life as best we could. The staff were too busy for such childish nonsense and questions were answered with a silent rebuff, or worse, a sudden smack for being a nuisance. The staff had no time for a child's sobbing. I clammed up because it was safer. I coped as best I could."

Noel started his day in a dormitory of twenty

children, their cast iron cots lined up in two straight rows with the bed-wetters separated at one end. At seven o'clock he joined the throngs of children heading to the dining room for breakfast. They lined up in front of large buckets of gluggy porridge and served themselves one scoop with a long handled ladle.

At the table, the children stood to attention to say grace before hungrily devouring their food. When he was older, Noel was given the job of getting up early to stoke the boiler and cut the wood before breakfast; a job he loved.

After breakfast the children went to the school room where they sat in desks in long rows in unheated class rooms despite Ballarat's cold climate where winter temperatures could drop to as low as three degrees Celsius with overnight lows of minus five degrees Celsius. Alan Radcliffe, in his submission to the Senate Inquiry, recalls suffering from the cold at Ballarat Orphanage to the point of getting chilblains on his 'ears, fingers and toes'.

The children were drilled in the basics of spelling and the multiplication tables. As was the custom in Victorian schools at the time, reading was taught using the *Victorian Readers*, one for each year. The *Readers* included poems such as *The Owl and the Pussy Cat*, fairy tales and other stories including *The*

Hobyahs. I can imagine what might have been in the minds of the Orphanage children when they read *The Three Wishes* in the Third Book.

Teachers could choose to inflict punishment, such as 'the cuts' or a caning, on children who did not spell words correctly or gave wrong answers to their times tables. However, Noel remembers his teacher as being patient and caring. She would sit beside him if he did not understand something and explain it to him.

At midday, the children stopped for lunch, which was usually a hot meal such as stewed rabbit, followed by steamed pudding or other dessert. The staff watched the children to make sure they ate all the food put in front of them. One day, when Noel refused to eat his steamed pudding, a staff member pushed his head down onto his plate and slammed his face into the sticky pudding. Noel retaliated by picking up the plate of steamed pudding and throwing it at the man. After that, Noel was not forced to eat pudding he did not like.

The school day ended at 3.30 p.m. Then there was work to be done. The children worked in the vegetable garden or the pigsty, chopped wood for the boiler and milked the cows. The tradition of hard working orphans was established early at Ballarat Orphanage where 'every boy and girl is taught to work, first in the way of cleanliness and order. ...Girls will, by the time they leave the orphanage, be good plain cooks, they will be able to make their own clothes and will understand all about laundry.' *(The Argus,* 1929.)

Noel's evening meal at five o'clock was usually bread and butter with jam or treacle and a cup of milky tea. Orphanage children often had to endure the mouth-watering aroma of delicious food served to the staff while they forced down their mass produced fare.

At bed time, the children were sent to their dormitories which, like the school room, were unheated. After warning the children not to wet the bed, the staff patrolled the corridors alert for any child breaking the rules by talking. If caught, the guilty child was made to stand by their bed for ten to fifteen minutes, shivering with cold.

Violence was another hazard faced by the children at Ballarat Orphanage. Noel remembers retaliating against staff members who used physical violence. According to Frank Golding, most of the staff at the Orphanage used physical intimidation. In his submission to the Senate Inquiry he recalls: 'Charlie McGregor, the head 'carer', set the tone. Not a day went by without him wielding his waddy, banging heads together, dishing out a backhander, a slap across the lug, or a box over the ears. Even the toddlers knew to keep out of the way of his vile stick. The schoolyard was his point of ambush. McGregor stood at the gateway with yard broom at the ready for those who were slow in coming out. Over the years many a broom handle broke over a kid's back or bum. The quickest children avoided him. The slowest bore the brunt. We all feared and loathed him.'

Sexual abuse of children in orphanages, including Ballarat Orphanage, has now been well documented. Staff and older boys would take advantage of vulnerable young boys who were desperate for affection. The other boys lived in dread of it happening to them. Golding writes: '…whenever sexual abuse happened, I felt grubby because there seemed no good reason that it wasn't me.'

Luckily, Noel escaped sexual abuse at Ballarat Orphanage. He recalls an approach by a staff member on one occasion but he took defensive action by running away and, on passing a line of football boots, picked one up and threw it at the man. He was a kid who was ready to fight and therefore not a soft target for an abuser. Perhaps that is why he was spared this betrayal, at least.

For Noel too, no-one came. He says it did not bother him because he did not know any better. However, some children felt the pain of loss on visiting days and would go off on their own and watch, unseen, the other children with their parents. Some, like Lorraine Rodgers, who was at Ballarat Orphanage the same time as Noel, 'would go in hiding, so no-one would know that I was crying'. (Submission to *Senate Inquiry*.)

Noel does remember one visitor when he was around ten years old; a lady who called herself Aunty Marj and gave him a copy of *Gullivers Travels*. I would like to think that this was Myrtle posing as Noel's aunty but I cannot imagine how, given our family financial situation and her commitments as a wife and mother, she would have been able to travel from Orbost to Ballarat. She had a friend who lived in Lydiard Street, Ballarat and they corresponded regularly so perhaps, assuming Myrtle even knew where Noel was, her friend took the book to him. On the other hand, it might have been a relative on his father's side.

Like his sister Audrey, Noel suffered the disappointment of just missing out on being adopted. The owners of the milk bar in Queenscliffe where the children from Ballarat Orphanage spent their summer holidays had a son the same age as Noel. The two boys got on well and the family sometimes took Noel on holidays with them to Mildura. When Noel was thirteen they decided to adopt him. Unfortunately, he was only six weeks into his six month probation period when the family circumstances changed as a result of an accident. Adoption plans had to be shelved. Noel was sent back to the Orphanage. His adoption did not seem to be subject to his father's approval as was the case with Audrey. It is possible the superintendent of Ballarat Orphanage was deemed his legal guardian because his father had not paid the mandatory maintenance. Orphanage records state: 'The father paid the maintenance for about three months and left the state. The Police and our Solicitor have been unable to contact him.'

Agnes Bishop appears to have aided and abetted her son in his deception of Ballarat Orphanage. In 1948, in response to an official registered letter from the Orphanage's solicitors addressed to Henry Bishop, she wrote: 'I am returning it to you as he hasn't lived here for some considerable time, about two years.' The information she supplied in the letter was probably true but the implication was that she did not know where he was living and that was certainly not true. Ultimately, her efforts to conceal the whereabouts of her son were in vain because in 1948, the Ballarat Orphanage managed to locate Henry Bishop through the Albury Police.

Faced with the possibility of having to fight criminal charges for unpaid maintenance, he wrote to the

Orphanage, apparently to come to an arrangement in respect to his debt and future payments. The contents of this letter reveal the spineless nature of Henry Bishop. He justifies his negligence in not making payments by claiming that 'my wife deserted me and my children while I was in the army and I just had to do the best I could under the circumstances.' That makes my blood boil, not only because the claim that Myrtle deserted her children is untrue but because no self respecting man in the 1940s would use his wife as an excuse for anything even if she were at fault. If he had any sense of decency he would simply not have mentioned it. To hide behind a false claim about her is downright cowardly. He further excuses his actions in not making payments with: 'I have since been married and I have two young children and my eldest son to keep. I am just an ordinary painter and I do not collect any fancy wage and besides I have to live and pay rent.'

Although he claims in the letter that 'I will do my best to wipe off the debt', it appears to have been a delaying tactic. According to the Orphanage records, Henry Bishop left the address in Brisbane where they had managed to locate him and they 'have heard nothing since'.

Of course, Noel was unaware of all this. In fact, he did not even know his parents were alive and was not aware he had a brother and a sister. Noel, Audrey and Bertie were all unaware that many kilometres away their mother was alive and well with a new family and a new husband.

Chapter 17

BY 1963 MY FATHER'S ILLNESS had advanced considerably. He lost weight and his dark, tanned skin started to take on a yellow hue and there was a gauntness about him. The optimism, confidence and the hint of mischief that had characterised him were no longer there. My mother probably noticed that his sleeping patterns had changed; how he tossed and turned. Perhaps she sometimes awoke in the middle of the night to find his side of the bed empty and the sheet damp and clammy from perspiration.

Nevertheless, my parents took care to make sure their children's lives continued as much as possible in the normal way. We were hardly aware that Dad was sick and certainly had no inkling that his illness was serious. Apart from anything else, Mum and Dad were both of the generation that believed children did not need to be burdened with what was happening in the adult world. We did not hear either of them complain and, as was her habit, my mother used cheerfulness and laugher to hide her emotions. Dad continued working, although it must have been extremely difficult for him to do so.

The pressure on my parents was made worse because, although I did not realise it at the time, Nan also started to show signs of ill health about a year after we moved in. I do not know the nature of her illness but she was in her seventies so presumably it was something age related. She started to spend more time in her room resting and was quieter than usual. My mother became more concerned about any noise we made.

Inevitably there was tension in our home. Bobby and Maxie were entering adulthood. Maxie had become moody and refused to sleep in the same room as his brother. He was now sleeping in the dining room, the room that had once been kept in pristine condition for Sunday lunch and Christmas Day. The twins fought with each other daily. They had also moved to another bedroom. Well, it was really just a section of the back veranda that my father had partitioned off for them. I had entered the self-absorbed moody teenage stage and that must have been particularly difficult for the adults to deal with. It is no wonder that the noisy, unsettled brood in the household tested the patience of both my parents and Nan.

One wet afternoon we were all 'cooped up inside'. My sister Irene was with Mum, watching her breastfeed the baby. This was also one of the intimacies I enjoyed with my mother as a young child. Another was brushing her long hair in the evenings. She was patient and loving in the way she suffered my clumsy yanks and pulls at her hair. Eventually, she taught my young hands how to handle the brush without hurting her and I would give her hair one hundred smooth strokes.

On this particular day, I was in the kitchen with the twins while Nan was preparing the vegetables for the evening meal. Mum and Nan shared the cooking but when Mum 'had her hands full with the baby' Nan would usually cook tea for all of us. Kevin and Georgie, who were around ten years old at the time, were playing a board game called *Snakes and Ladders*. It was a game I liked playing but on this occasion I had been delegated to supervise the twins and keep them occupied. As usual, Kevin and Georgie were arguing with each other.

"You landed on the snake. You have to go down."

"I did not. I was here."

Georgie moved his die back to the square it had been on previously, according to his reckoning.

"If I move five spaces I get to here."

He placed the die one square before the top of the

snake.

"You weren't there," said Kevin.

"I was so."

"You liar! You were here. Tell him, June."

"I was not. You're stupid. Tell him, June. He's stupid."

"June," said Nan, who had her back to us at the sink where she was working her way through a mountain of potatoes, expertly peeling them with her kitchen knife. "Keep those kids quiet. I can't hear myself think."

"Stop it, you two," I said. "You'll have to start the game all over again now."

"That's not fair. I was winning."

"Were not. I was."

"Shut your gob."

"Shut your big fat gob."

"Shut your cake-hole."

"That's enough. I'm packing up the board. You can go and play somewhere else."

I began packing up the game. Kevin started yelling at me. Georgie started crying.

"Now look what you've done," said Nan.

"It's not my fault. I shouldn't have to look after these bloody babies."

"We're not babies!"

Nan turned from the sink.

"That's no way for a young lady to talk," she said sharply, drying her hands on her apron.

"I don't care. I wish they weren't my brothers. I hate brothers!"

"That's enough!"

Her sharp tone stung me. I had a close relationship with Nan from spending many happy hours with her in the kitchen. Any indication that she did not love me cut me to the quick, sensitive child that I was. I felt warm tears welling and got up from the table, ready to storm from the room.

"You're always picking on me," I yelled at her.

"What nonsense," scoffed Nan, reaching for a saucepan to put the peeled potatoes in. "Now leave your brothers alone and go and do something useful."

This curt dismissal was too much for my breaking heart to bear. The tears started to roll down my cheeks but I turned my head quickly so that no one could see. Like my brothers, I viewed crying as a sign of weakness. Since Nan was, in my eyes, deliberately trying to hurt me and picking on me for no good reason the appropriate response was to hit back. I wiped away the tears, took a deep breath to prevent any trace of tremor entering my voice and turned to face her with fury steaming from every pore of my skin.

"I hate you!" I yelled.

Quickly turning my back on her, I yanked at the door handle. The saucepan Nan had been holding became a projectile. It connected painfully with my heel as I escaped through the kitchen door, slamming it hard behind me. I raced around to the side of the veranda, curled up in a corner under an overhanging plant and bawled my eyes out. As I often did during this period of my development, I sank into a mire of melancholy. The whole world was against me. No-one cared about me.

Poor Nan. The adult me can look back and appreciate what a terrible thing that was to say to her especially after she had so generously taken us all in, cooked for us, played with us and allowed her house to be taken over.

I regret to say that I once also yelled such spiteful words at my mother. It was when we were still living out on the Bonang. I was around five or six years old and was angry at being thwarted by her authority. In my frustration, I stamped my foot and spat out the words with childish fury in each syllable.

"I hate you. You're the worst mother in the whole wide world."

Her face blanched. Anguish swamped her soft hazel eyes. Her hands gripped the edges of her apron as though she was trying to rip it from her body. I knew I had scored a bull's eye. The sense of satisfaction this gave me extinguished my anger. Yet my defiant triumph collapsed as I watched my mother. She closed her eyes and quickly turned away, busying herself at the kitchen sink. There was no indication of anger, no slamming down of pots or cutlery. Her movements were slow, methodical and quiet.

This reaction startled me. She was used to my childish tantrums and usually just laughed indulgently or calmly ignored me. I had never seen her react this way before. The warm invisible thread that connected me to my mother had been inexplicably severed to be replaced by a cold void. Fear held me captive. I did not fully understand. I only knew that somehow my words had torpedoed into a vulnerable place within my mother. It frightened me to realise that the source of my security could have a weakness that allowed her to be toppled like the lofty trees of the forest that swayed and crashed to the ground when they were felled by my father's axe.

I wished anger had been her reaction. Her anger, which erupted when I tested her to breaking point, was something I understood and expected. She might grab my skinny arm and slap my bottom with her hand. If I was quick enough to escape her grasp she gave chase, sometimes pursuing me around the house with a broom or a saucepan. If I managed to get out the back door and down the steps before she caught me, I knew I was safe. She never chased any of us beyond the back steps.

Her anger never frightened me but this silent withdrawal terrified me. I stood watching her back. My eyes took in her pretty brown hair coiled up at the neck, her shoulder blades moving under the floral cotton of her dress as she arranged plates on the draining board, her slim waist with the strings of her apron tied at the back, her bare legs and flat slippers. I breathed in the musky smell of her talcum powder. She was as familiar as she had always been. Yet, I knew she was not the same. Confusion filled my child brain. Several long minutes passed. Outside, cockatoos screeched across the sky.

Finally, I left the kitchen and headed for my usual sanctuary, the hayshed at the far end of the back yard, clambering over the rectangular bales of hay inside to make my way up to the top. Once there, I crawled into a gap between two bales and decided to stay there forever.

Later, Mum retrieved me from the hayshed. She stood outside and called my name. She always did this, called to me from outside rather than coming into the hayshed. It was as though she did not wish to intrude in my private world. Her voice revealed no hint of hostility or coldness but I was hesitant about facing her and climbed down out of the hay reluctantly.

Emerging into the sunlight, I took slow steps toward her, head bowed, not wanting to look into her eyes. I knew I was guilty of a grave offence even though I could not fathom exactly what it was. When I reached my mother, she rested her arm lightly on my shoulders as we walked back to the house. Her warmth embraced me. I inhaled the closeness of her and heard her words, softly spoken.

"It's all right, love," she said.

She had the merciful wisdom of a caring mother and recognised that I had no understanding of the pain I had caused her.

Likewise, the teenage me that had been so hurtful to Nan had no understanding of the seriousness of our family's situation. I was not aware that my grandmother was ill and my father was dying. Not only that, but I was at the stage when I was the only important person in the world. Yet, I did not seem to be important to my parents anymore. I was able to come and go more or less as I pleased. While my friends' parents imposed curfews on them when we went riding on our bikes or for picnics along the creek, Mum and Dad did not. I took this as a sign of their neglect and lack of caring. Now, of course, I realise that they had so much on their minds and were in such deep despair about their situation that minor details like what time I returned from daytime excursions with my friends must have seemed inconsequential.

During this period we also saw more of my father's temper than we had ever done. His anger was fearsome in action but was usually slow to kindle. However, his illness and no doubt our crowded living conditions meant that his tolerance was frequently stretched to breaking point. Discipline of the day was 'the strap' administered across the buttocks or backs of the legs. As a rule, Dad used this only as a last resort and more often on the boys than on me or my sister. However, he now used it more often on all of us, including me.

Oblivious to the stress that the adults in the house were under I was concerned only about myself. I have no doubt I pushed them to the limit of their forbearance. As a result, my father sometimes felt it was necessary to give me a good hiding. I saw this as a serious betrayal because he had always been gentle and caring and generous spirited toward me. So, in order to punish him for punishing me, I would refuse to cry when he strapped me. This was a bit silly because whenever any of us started to cry when he was using the strap on us he would always stop.

However, using flawed childish logic, I reasoned that if he couldn't make me cry he would think he had not hurt me. That would be my revenge. Perhaps that was also Audrey's attitude to the nun who tried to 'break her'.

One day I decided to be particularly stubborn. Dad had brought his belt across my legs several times and red welts had formed. However, I kept my mouth firmly shut and my eyes dry until his belt accidentally caught on an ornament I had hanging on the wall. It was something I had won in a competition and meant a lot to me because of that. The ornament, made of porcelain, smashed into pieces when it hit the floor. I burst into tears. My father stopped belting me immediately. With tears streaming down my face, I directed an accusatory stare at him. He looked a little non-plussed, as if he couldn't understand why the breaking of a worthless little trinket could cause me to wail like a banshee when his physical punishment could not. I saw the anger in his eyes dissipate to be replaced by something else; regret, I think. Not regret that he had given me a good hiding because he never belted us without cause, but perhaps regret that he had allowed his anger to control the length and intensity of the beating.

There must have been some sort of cut off point

in our ages when a good hiding was no longer considered appropriate punishment because Bobby was around eighteen or nineteen when he missed out on a hiding despite having committed what in my parents' eyes was a disgraceful transgression.

He was working at one of the local sawmills and took his cheque to a local shop to cash it. It was not unusual in those days for a shopkeeper to cash a wage cheque for someone they knew. In Bobby's case it was more because they knew Dad. Anyway, on this occasion Bobby, who was by now tall, dark and handsome like his father, saw an opportunity to get some more money. Australia's currency at the time was 'pounds, shillings and pence'. Bobby had a cheque for nine pounds but he made some simple alterations to the words and figures in the cheque, so that when he presented it at the shop it had miraculously metamorphosed into a cheque for ninety pounds. He might not have intended to keep the money for himself; it is possible that it was a naive effort to get money for the family.

I am sure he thought it was a foolproof plan without serious consequences. However, being his first attempt at forgery, Bobby's efforts were easily detected. The shopkeeper called the police and they contacted our father. I can only imagine the shame that Dad must have suffered. He did not have money or status. The one thing he did have was respect. His family on his mother's side as well as his father's side had been in the area since the late 1800s and were respected and well known. Dad had carried on the family tradition of respect and honour. His reputation in the community was dear to him. The shopkeeper, probably as a courtesy to our father, did not press charges but Bobby was not home free. He still had to endure Dad's rage.

"If you weren't too old, I'd give you the biggest thrashing you have ever had in your life. You wouldn't be able to stand up afterwards for days."

Those were the words that began a fierce and degrading tongue lashing for Bobby. If my father had only realised the power of his verbal punishment he would probably have used it more often. He had the ability to express the full force of his anger in his eyes and to make his tone so cold that you suddenly felt as if he had cut you out of his life and had never been your father. Bobby hung his head and cowered like a frightened animal. Later, I heard my father talking to my mother about the incident.

"It's a good job he got caught," he said. "It'll teach him a lesson. He'll think twice before he does anything like that again."

I'm not sure that getting caught and having to face the police was the stronger deterrent in this case.

My father's wrath, scorn and contempt for his actions probably had a deeper impact on my brother.

The worry of his teenage children growing increasingly recalcitrant, the anxiety of his own illness and the added concern of knowing his mother was ill must have created overwhelming stress for Dad.

One day in April 1963, Nan became so ill that Mum called the ambulance to take her to the Orbost Hospital. Unfortunately, Nan passed away before the ambulance reached its destination. Although Nan's ill health had been a strain for both my parents, they mourned the passing of this kind and generous lady.

Chapter 18

MYRTLE WAS STILL GRIEVING THE death of her mother-in-law and trying to cope with the responsibility of seven lively children while burdened with the knowledge that her husband was unlikely to recover from his illness when she received an unexpected visitor.

By this time, her first three children Bertie, Audrey and Noel were adults. Bertie was 24 years old, had moved out of home and started work. He had dreamed of one day being a surgeon or a pilot. Unfortunately, the family did not have the money to help him realise his dreams. Instead, he had been enrolled in a technical college.

Like his brother, Noel also had dreams for his future which he was unable to pursue. He wanted to be a scientist but was told by the superintendent at Ballarat Orphanage that he had to attend the local technical college. Noel stuck it out for eighteen months but eventually left to get a job at Myttons

Ltd, a local cutlery manufacturer. Ballarat Orphanage was no longer his home as he had moved into a hostel at the age of fifteen. He still had no inkling that he had a brother and a sister and no knowledge of his mother and seven half-siblings who were living in the same state of Victoria.

Audrey, now twenty two, had also left the orphanage where she had grown up. At the age of fifteen she became a mother's helper with the Rodgers family in Albury. She looked after the babies and did the housework but was not treated like a slave. They showed her the same respect and love as any other member of the family. Not surprisingly, Audrey was happy living there.

When Audrey's term as mother's helper to Eileen Rodgers came to a close, Audrey did not want to leave the Rodgers family and return to the orphanage. Had she been sent back she might have stayed at the orphanage as part of the staff for the rest of her life as some of the girls did. Instead, she continued on with the Rodgers family where she remained for approximately four years.

Eileen Rodgers, who was the closest Audrey came to having a mother, earned a warm place in her heart. However, Audrey's burning desire to know her family, which had been with her all her life, remained strong. Through her paternal grandmother, she found out her father was living in Ipswich. The Rodgers family did everything they could to help Audrey become reunited with her biological family. Eileen Rodgers' brother drove her from Albury to her father's house in Ipswich, a distance of over 1300 kilometres. Here, Audrey was reunited with her brother, Bertie, after more than fifteen years. Neither of them knew about their younger brother, Noel.

Audrey stayed with Henry Bishop and his second wife in Ipswich although she was not entirely happy there. After a couple of years, she made her way to Sydney in NSW. She was an attractive young woman with an interest in fashion which was reflected in her elegant dress style. No doubt these attributes helped her land a job with David Jones Ltd, a well known Australian department store. In the 1960s, Audrey worked in their glove department and in later years in the shoe department before moving into the hospitality industry. During this time, Audrey intensified her search for her mother. Eventually, she found out Myrtle's address from Etti Webb and began writing to her in Orbost although Myrtle did not reply to her letters.

When Audrey set off to travel around Australia with a boyfriend she decided to include the small township of Orbost in their itinerary. Myrtle did not know that her eldest daughter was about to knock on her door. Orbost has only one main street where the shops are located so it was not difficult for Audrey and her boyfriend to find their way around. They asked for directions from the local shopkeepers and arrived at 61 Salisbury Street, which was only 500 metres away, sometime after lunch. I am sure Audrey's expectations of this meeting were high. All her life she had yearned for a mother. She was about to be reunited with the woman who had given birth to her and nurtured her through her first tender years.

The conditions were not ideal for this meeting. Apart from being unannounced, Audrey had her boyfriend with her. Perhaps this was a conscious choice to provide her with support for a meeting that must have filled her with apprehension and anxiety. What do you say to your mother after so many years of separation? Apart from the awkwardness of not knowing how to relate to her, she might have feared her mother would reject her. That would have been too great a trauma to face alone. As it turned out, her mother did not reject her. Yet their reunion must have fallen far short of Audrey's expectations.

Myrtle invited Audrey and her boyfriend in.

"Would you like a cup of tea, love?" she said.

Offering a cup of tea was the usual ice-breaker in country areas and it was familiar ground for Myrtle. I suspect this was her way of coping with what must have been quite a shock. Separated mothers often cannot face the trauma of meeting their children years after they have been taken from them.

Murray Legro from Ballarat whose mother was forced to give him up for adoption at six weeks of age spent years searching for his birth mother. When he finally located her, the idea of meeting her estranged son as an adult was too much for his mother.

'We had four letters, two phone calls,' he writes on the website *ABC Open: Separated*, 'then her sister rang up and said she can't handle it, so I backed off.'

Despite the potentially unfavourable conditions, Myrtle and Audrey spent a pleasant afternoon together although no serious issues were discussed. Audrey told Myrtle about her work and her plans for the future. Myrtle listened and laughed and joked with her. It was getting close to 3 p.m. when Myrtle stood up and hinted that it was time for Audrey and her boyfriend to leave because the children would be 'getting home from school soon'.

I can only imagine the hurt Audrey must have experienced when her mother said this. She could never have envisaged that the joyous, yearned for reunion with her mother would end in such a way. It also shocked me to discover that Mum could have been so apparently insensitive. I was even more bewildered by the fact that she had not taken this opportunity to welcome her daughter back into her life. I remained mystified until I started to research the lives of other women who had had to give up their children.

One of the many publications that helped me to understand how Mum was able to cope with her situation was *Silent Violence: Australia's White Stolen Children*, a thesis by Merryl Moor of Griffith University. I was interested to read the following quote from 'a Sydney birthmother and researcher' in Moor's thesis: '...The loss of a living part of oneself creates in the mother a level of trauma and anxiety so great that the mother must manifest a false self in order to survive. The experience essentially becomes 'something that happened to someone I used to be'. The mother blocks the experience ... She remains suspended and, therefore, silent unless a trigger event occurs and forces her mind to face her loss.'

This fits very well with what happened to my mother. The loss of her first three children became something that happened to someone she used to be. With her other self locked away in some lonely abyss, her false self was able to live a full and productive life as a 'normal' mother.

This might also explain why Myrtle discontinued her attempts to keep in touch with her children when they were young. She would not have known where Bertie was after he moved to Queensland and she probably did not know where Noel was but she did know where Audrey was. She was an excellent and regular letter writer. Why didn't she write to her daughter? Was it because that part of her life had to remain locked away in order for her to cope?

When the first letter had arrived from the adult Audrey, Myrtle must have had to face her past and the secret she had kept under psychological lock and key. I feel sure that she would have done some soul searching. Her false self must have been threatened. The thought of having to face her loss and having to reveal her secret would have been too traumatic to bear. She would have had to confront the shame and guilt and possibly self loathing she felt because she had not been a mother to her three children. Her feelings would have been similar to other mothers forcibly separated from their children who, in the words of a mother quoted in the Moor thesis, 'suffered feelings of never being a good enough person or mother to my other children'.

Another mother, Jenny, whose story is recorded in *Releasing the Past: Mothers' stories of their stolen babies*, reflects that she was 'Burdened by a deep sense of worthlessness, of not deserving or belonging in my own good life, my constant fear was that of losing those I loved – a fear that they, too, would be snatched away.'

This is a fear Myrtle would have lived with; the fear that revealing her secret might result in the loss of her new family. She risked losing the love and respect of the children she now had. Like Jenny, she probably also had a fear, irrational but nevertheless real to her, that her children would be taken from her as her first children had been. A deep rooted fear of losing her subsequent children was something a separated mother often had to live with.

Also on the website *ABC Open: Separated*, is the story of Julienne; a mother whose baby had been taken from her at birth: 'I lived in constant fear of critical neighbours and teachers who might be instrumental in the removal of the children of my marriage.'

For all of these reasons and perhaps more, Myrtle changed the word 'Mother' to 'Aunty' on the letters and postcards Audrey sent her. I found several of them in her papers after her death. Audrey had addressed them as 'Dear Mother' but Myrtle had written over the word 'Mother' and altered it to 'Aunty'. This simple change meant that she was able to keep her false self intact without actually rejecting Audrey. I believe that in her mind she became Audrey's aunty. When Audrey arrived at her home that afternoon, Myrtle met her not as her mother but as her aunt.

On the day Audrey arrived to be reunited with her mother I was at Orbost High School, only a block away from our house. Yet the sister I did not know existed, had come and gone without me even knowing. Once again, Myrtle proved to be an expert at keeping her secret. My father, by now only doing light duties, was at work the afternoon Audrey came. I suspect my mother did not tell him about her daughter's visit given his state of health and the fact that her secret was probably never discussed after they left Albury in 1944.

Audrey continued to write to Myrtle but her mother did not respond even though Audrey pleaded with her to write back. However, when I went through Myrtle's documents after her death I came across the photos Audrey had sent of herself as well as several slips of paper with Audrey's various Sydney addresses written on them in Mum's handwriting. Did she intend (or want) to write to Audrey or did keeping her letters, photos and details of where she lived help Myrtle to maintain a connection with her daughter from a safe distance?

Chapter 19

DURING THE MONTHS THAT FOLLOWED Audrey's visit, my father's health continued to deteriorate. In July 1964 he was admitted to the Alfred Hospital in Melbourne for tests and blood transfusions. He returned home in August but was readmitted on September 11, 1964 and remained there for almost three weeks. This separation was difficult for Mum and Dad.

I found two unused Alfred Hospital visitor cards in Mum's papers. These cards allowed her to visit Dad 'between 3 p.m. and 4 p.m. on Wednesdays and Sundays only'. However, it was almost impossible for her to visit him. There was no passenger train from Melbourne to Orbost. The line ended at Bairnsdale ninety kilometres away. A journey to Melbourne meant a 60-90 minute car drive to Bairnsdale, perhaps longer depending on the condition of the road at that time, followed by a long train journey of approximately five hours. Even if she could afford it, having young children at home would have made such a journey problematic. Although we did have the telephone on at home, calls to Melbourne were expensive. The best Mum and Dad could do was to write to each other every day.

In his letter to Mum of September 17, 1964, Dad responds to one of her letters with:

> *Yes, Myrtle, I miss you a lot, too, but what can I do? It's in the doctors' hands and they don't tell you much...Now look Myrtle, you want to look after yourself and don't sit up at night because I'm quite all right. As a matter of fact I feel pretty good, but I still sweat at night and I get a temp now and again. Now, you get some sleep and don't worry. They'll probably get sick of me before long. I hope so anyway. I weigh 10:10. That was last Sunday but I think I have put on some now because they are giving me vitamin tablets and I am eating pretty well. I better go now. Keep writing Myrtle. I look forward to your letters. Look after yourself. Love from George.* XXXXXXXXXXXXXX (10:10 or 10 stone: 10 pounds, is equal to 150 lbs or just over 68kg)

On September 21 he writes with obvious excitement that he is coming home and asks that Bobby or Maxie meet him at Bairnsdale Station:

It's Monday today. Three days and I will be on the train home, I hope, anyway. Dr Paul told me that and Sister also told me, so I think it will be all right.

He repeats his plea for Mum to go to bed early telling her it 'does you no good up all night'. The letter continues:

Got plenty of money still, Myrtle? Not that I could give you any if you didn't have but just thought I would ask. Tell Peter I'll be home on Friday. Funny he should miss me so much.

My youngest brother Peter was only four years old at this time and missed his father deeply when he was in hospital. Dad's next letter to Mum was on Friday, September 25, 1964.

Dear Myrtle,

I'm sorry I couldn't make it to Bairnsdale today but it wasn't my fault – some misunderstanding with the doctors. Anyway, Dr Standish said you rang up and that you met the train in Bairnsdale. You couldn't of got the telegram telling you I wasn't coming. Sister said she would send you one this morning but apparently they missed out somewhere along the line. Anyway, I have to get another blood transfusion in the morning and then if the Head Doctor is satisfied with me I will be home about Monday or Tuesday morning so that would be all right. If you have enough money I will hold this cheque until then, but if it's any longer I'll have to trust the mail and send it back. I suppose you're tired after your wait for nothing at Bairnsdale. Well, I was pretty annoyed about it myself, I can tell you. But it's for my own good I suppose. As long as you lot up there are alright, that's the main thing.

The cheque he refers to is a Social Services cheque which was possibly an allowance he received because of his inability to earn an income through illness. It would have required his signature in order for Mum to access the money.

He goes on to describe an incident in the hospital when the doctors and nurses worked hard for over an hour to save a man but were unable to do so in the end. He praises the hard work of the medical staff saying, 'They sure work, these doctors.'

He finishes the letter as follows:

Anyway, I should be on Tuesday's train but as yet I am not sure. See you soon, Myrtle, and it can't be soon enough for me. I miss you too much. All my love. See you, Myrtle. From George. XXXXXXXX

In his next letter he wrote:

Dear Myrtle,

I am still here. There has been a mistake made. I can't go today after all. Dr Paul said I could and Dr Standish said I can't and it looks like Dr Standish must have won because I am still here. I could not write until late because I was kept waiting until three o'clock in the afternoon. I don't know if you got a telegram or not, but you were supposed to – about 9 o'clock this morning. Anyway, I am not sure what to do with this Social Services cheque. If I sign it and it gets lost in the mail, it's an open cheque. I don't know why they are keeping me. I'm alright. All I am doing is taking tablets. I reckon I could do this at home, I'm sure. However, the head doctor has just examined me so maybe that will decide them. It shouldn't be much longer – would like to get it back to you – this cheque, I mean.

Sorry, Myrtle, I couldn't get home today but it was out of my hands. I have been sitting around all day in my clothes and I still haven't got an answer. They thought I might catch the seven o'clock train but it doesn't look like it now. Anyhow, I will just have to leave it to them, I suppose. I haven't much choice in the matter it seems. I was always unlucky. Have you got any money to carry on a couple more days or not? If not, I'll just have to take the risk and send this cheque.

Two or three went out today. I don't know why they did not let me go today when they said they were going to. It mucks everyone up. So I won't bother to ask them anymore. What's the use when they give you the wrong date? I could have blown the place up.

Anyway, keep going if you can, Myrtle, and don't worry, I won't be long, I hope. So long, Myrtle. Write straight back. All my love. George. XXX

Dad was not released from hospital until five days later on September 30. However, his stay at home was brief. He was admitted to the local hospital in Orbost two months later. By this time he and Mum must have realised that he would not live for much longer. It was common knowledge in Orbost that if a seriously ill person was sent home from a Melbourne hospital and was not yet well they had been sent home to spend their last days with their family.

It was uncanny to see Dad quiet and listless. He did not eat much although Mum tried her best to tempt him with his favourite dishes. We had to be very quiet in the house and Mum sent us outside to play much of the time. As the weeks passed we saw less of him because he spent a lot of time sleeping.

How Mum managed to find the time and money

to give us kids a 'normal' Christmas that year I do not know, but she did. Bobby and Maxie had left home by this time to find work in other places but there were still five of us, the youngest being four-year-old Peter. Dad usually got our Christmas tree from the bush. He would chop off a branch of the Cherry Ballard, a cypress-like tree with soft green branches that reminded me of a willow tree. The small red berries of this native cherry were gathered for eating by the Aboriginal people who loved their sharp taste. I don't remember who got our Christmas tree that year but we had a lovely one. It stood in the bay window. Mum kept us busy for days making decorations from coloured paper to put on the tree.

"Let's make it look extra special to give your father a surprise on Christmas morning," she said.

On Christmas Eve she got us to bed early as she always did by telling us that we had to be fast asleep before Santa arrived. He would know if we were awake and he would not enter the house with the presents. Even though I had serious doubts about the existence of Santa Claus, I went along with the subterfuge as I always did. It was part of the excitement and the ritual. That night I heard the rustling of wrapping paper as I lay in my bed pretending to be asleep. Mum might have had some presents already wrapped but she probably spent hours wrapping presents for us that night.

I awoke in the morning to the sounds of Georgie and Kevin fighting with each other; each accusing the other of trying to open the brightly wrapped parcels. They always fought with each other on Christmas morning. It was reassuring to hear this sign of normality.

When we were all out of bed, we opened up our presents with the usual noisy frenzy. Dad, pale and thin, reminded me of Pop as he sat quietly watching us. When Mum tried to tell us to be quiet he shook his head.

"It's all right, Mum," he said. "It's Christmas."

Although I did not realise it at the time, the unspoken message was 'It's my last Christmas with them'. He would have known by then that he was unlikely to see another year out.

When the excitement was over, Mum shooed the younger kids outside to play.

"And don't make too much noise," she called after them. "Your father needs to have a rest before dinner."

While Dad was sleeping and the kids were playing, I helped Mum in the kitchen. As in most Australian homes at the time, we always had a heavy, cooked meal for Christmas lunch no matter what the weather. It was a meal more suited for a

Northern Hemisphere winter than a hot Australian summer but it was a tradition brought over from Britain in the early days of colonisation. So, like other Australian mothers of the time, Mum sweltered for hours in a hot kitchen with the wood stove well stoked and a hot oven ready.

Our main course of turkey, chicken, roast vegetables and peas was followed by plum pudding with cream and jelly. Mum always made the traditional plum pudding in a cloth with sixpences inside and had it ready and hanging several weeks before Christmas. We all loved plum pudding and yelled with delight when we found a sixpence in the piece on our plate. Christmas dinner that year was the same raucous event as it always was. We blew whistle streamers, nudged and shouted at each other, fought over our sixpences and ate every morsel that was put in front of us. Dad sat in his usual place at the head of the table and carved the turkey and the chicken. He smiled at us from time to time but he was mostly quiet and sometimes seemed to have trouble breathing. He ate very little and Mum helped him back to bed before we had finished our jelly and ice cream.

The next day the ambulance came and took Dad back to Orbost Hospital. Mum visited him at every opportunity which was usually two or three times a day. He was in and out of the hospital during January 1965. Each time he came home he looked less like my father.

On Thursday 28 January when Mum went to visit Dad at the hospital, she stayed there all afternoon coming home only to see to our evening meal before returning to the hospital. She did not come back until later in the evening.

I recall my mother arriving home from the hospital and standing for a long time in the doorway looking across at us kids in the lounge room. We were absorbed in a television show and barely noticed her presence.

After a few moments, she spoke. "Your father died tonight."

We heard her heavy step along the hall to the room they had shared. Not knowing how to react or what to say, we sat in silence in front of the television. Mum was alone in her room that night.

Chapter 20

OUR SUMMER THAT YEAR WAS dry and hot. Fierce bushfires burned all around Orbost and a heavy drift of smoke covered East Gippsland. Lightning strikes started new fires in the tinder dry forests until all of Gippsland was ravaged by fire. Conditions were so severe that the train line was closed for a period and, for the first time since the 1959 fires, all timber activities in the Orbost district were shut down for a short period of time. Homes and shops were destroyed, thousands of stock perished, almost 10 000 hectares of grassland and over 200 000 hectares of bushland were burnt. The fires burned throughout February until mid March when rain finally arrived. The devastation would have been even worse had it not been for hundreds of fire-fighters and support volunteers who fought to control the fires and protect life and property.

While farmers, timber workers and householders were coping with heartbreaking losses as a result of the fires, Mum was coming to terms with the loss that had long been looming in her life. The death of Dad left her shattered. He had been the lynchpin, the driving force of our family. I feel sure his death also left Mum emotionally vulnerable. Her 'false self' had been supported by his presence. The role of George's wife was central to this other self and had enabled her to start her life again. Her fragility, coupled with her grief, must have put her in a state of despair, perhaps even depression. With all her family far away in Albury, she had no-one to offer her emotional support.

In a small community like Orbost there were many people offering practical assistance but she did not have a close friend or relative on whose shoulder she could cry; someone who might give her the strength to climb out of what was doubtless a dark and solitary place. We, her children, were all too young to understand what she was going through. Not only that, but our focus was on ourselves. Knowing my mother, I think that is the way she preferred it. She would not want us to bear her burden, or have adult troubles intrude on our innocence or our carefree existence.

Somehow, Mum managed to put aside her grief and loneliness and resume her role as mother; ensuring we were clean and fed and clothed and got to school on time each day. She made sure our routine was pretty much the same as before. Although her commitment to her family never wavered, Mum did withdraw after my father died. She did not have the emotional energy or perhaps even the physical stamina to maintain the same level of engagement with her kids and her home. This disengagement had started during the last months of my father's illness. It was as though she had entered a state of emotional numbness.

It must have seemed like an answer to a prayer when Cathy Solomon, a local Salvation Army member, appeared on our doorstep with her broad smile and arms open wide. Generous in body and generous in spirit, Cathy offered friendship and support to Myrtle when she needed it most.

Cathy is a local Aboriginal woman, a Kurnai woman. The Kurnai are the first people of the Gippsland area. In the 1960s some of the Aboriginal people lived in the township and there were also Aboriginal camps along the Snowy River near Orbost. At that time, many people in Australia, including people in Orbost, did not accept the Aboriginal people as equals; a legacy of the attitude and ignorance of the early English colonists who viewed all peoples who were not 'civilised' as less than human. However, there were Australians like my mother and father, who accepted people as equal human beings regardless of race, status or colour. I am grateful for that attitude legacy from my parents.

With succour and encouragement from Cathy, Myrtle gradually emerged from her grief. The two friends made regular trips between Orbost and Lakes Entrance, a distance of sixty kilometres, selling copies of the Salvation Army's magazine *The War Cry*. Mum would wander through the men's bar, rattling her money box at the drinkers, smiling and joking and charming them into buying copies. Those who pleaded lack of funds were quickly silenced with Myrtle's rejoinder.

"If you can afford to buy a beer, you can afford to buy a *War Cry*."

Sometimes Myrtle would be in the driver's seat on these trips, much to the apprehension of Cathy's sons because Myrtle's driving skills had not improved over the years. The boys rode in the back often covering their eyes with their hands as gum trees loomed close or appeared effortlessly and mysteriously in front of the car.

Initially, Myrtle's involvement with The Salvation Army was probably a distraction from her grief, her financial worries and the difficulties she faced in having to manage the family alone. Although Bobby and Maxie had left school and were now working,

Myrtle still had five of us to feed, clothe and put through school. It had always been important to her that her kids 'got a good education' and she wasn't about to let anything get in the way of that. However, she had debts to pay such as ambulance costs, other medical expenses and rates arrears. Child Endowment payments amounted to 10-15 shillings per week per child and her only other income was the War Widows' Pension. Even with generous assistance from the community she was not able to financially support herself and her children.

It would not have been an easy decision for her to make but she eventually sold the house in Salisbury Street. By 1969 she had moved into a Housing Commission house (public housing). A typical Housing Commission home at that time was a simple fibro house on cement blocks. Mum lived in Ralston Court, Orbost in an estate accommodating low income families.

By this time, Bobby, Maxie and I had left home to explore new horizons but Mum still had the twins, now teenagers, plus Irene and Peter living at home. With the help of kind individuals, her own determination and resourcefulness, she managed to take good care of all her children. Not only that, she sometimes looked after other mothers' babies when circumstances were difficult for them, such as when a mother was in hospital having another child, or simply when a mother found life with several children too difficult. She would also 'harbour' youths who had nowhere to live, offering them a place to sleep in an old caravan in her back yard as well as providing them with meals. There was always food available at her house for anyone who needed it.

As time went by, Myrtle became more and more involved with the Salvation Army where she found a supportive community and perhaps an escape from the pressures of her home life. She accepted the role of Sunday School teacher and was much loved by the children in her classes. Her Sunday School students and the neighbourhood kids were always welcome at her home. They were constantly visiting her, playing in her yard, enjoying the cakes she baked for them or simply sitting on the floor watching television with her.

Her friendship with Cathy remained strong. Apart from their church commitments, they enjoyed social activities together like swimming, walking and riding their bikes. Having fun with Cathy must have reminded Myrtle of happier times in Albury when, as young women, she and her cousins shared similar activities. I am sure her friendship with Cathy also contributed significantly toward her improved emotional strength.

Myrtle's social life gradually extended to the wider community within the Salvation Army. As her grieving subsided, her vivacious personality returned attracting the attentions of a male member of the church community. He had the same name as my father. Myrtle and the new George became close friends. She was not interested in anything more than friendship but, although their relationship was platonic, the new George remained by her side.

He must have been a source of strength for her at a time when she had a great deal to cope with. My brother, Kevin, for instance, despite being on medication to curb his epileptic seizures still sometimes suffered violent fits which worried Mum. The other children were often hard to control and Mum had difficulty disciplining them and struggled with their fluctuating moods. Dad had usually been the one to administer punishments for misdeeds but now Mum had to be the stern father as well as the nurturing mother.

Myrtle's friendship with George lasted several years. At one point marriage was mentioned, but soon after that George made the mistake of trying to help Myrtle discipline her kids. When, on one of my trips home from Melbourne, I asked Mum why George was not around anymore her mouth set in a determined line.

"Hhmpf! Telling me what to do with my kids! No-one comes between me and my kids," was her short answer.

Poor George probably had the best of intentions but he could not have known that her children would be an especially sensitive area. Any hint of outside intervention would have jarred like a drill on an exposed nerve. Although their closeness ended, Myrtle and George remained friends.

Throughout the 1970s, Myrtle continued to divide her time between home and the Salvation Army. She managed to steer the remainder of her children through their teenage years and into adulthood providing for them remarkably well given her circumstances. By this time I was living in Sydney where I met Dennis Barnes: a young man from England whom I later married. Dennis's parents had also migrated from England and were living in Melbourne with Dennis's brother, Brian, and sister, Anita.

In February 1971, I decided that Orbost would be a great halfway destination for Dennis and me to meet up with his parents who could meet my mother at the same time. Orbost was around seven hours by car from Sydney and four to five hours from Melbourne. Unfortunately, that was the year that the Snowy River, which floods on a regular basis along the rich alluvial river flats at Orbost, burst its banks in a spectacular way to create the worst floods on record.

A wall of water swamped the flats and swept everything in its path out to sea including sheep and cattle. Giant gum trees thirty metres tall were torn out by their roots and rolled along by the water. The Princes Highway Bridge over the Snowy River was destroyed. Consequently, like other visitors to the area, my new in-laws were stranded and could not return to Melbourne. Eventually, they were able to manoeuvre a way out of the area via a circuitous and perilous route and get back on the road to Melbourne.

For me, the floods were a welcome distraction because I was not comfortable about my husband and his family meeting Mum. Although I would not have acknowledged it or admitted it at the time, I realise now that I was ashamed of my mother's Housing Commission home and embarrassed by her lack of attention to housekeeping chores. I regret that I did not use the eyes of maturity to see instead, a woman and mother worthy of the highest respect.

The 1980s brought Mum joy as well as more tragedy. The joy arrived in the form of grandchildren. My sister Irene was by now in a relationship and in 1982 she gave birth to a girl. Mum was as excited about Sally's arrival as Irene was. That was the start of a strong, loving relationship between granddaughter and grandmother. Mum always had time to look after Sally, to encourage her development by reading to her, talking to her and playing with her.

Fourteen months after the birth of Sally tragedy struck when my brother, Kevin, was killed in a road accident in September 1983. When I arrived home for his funeral I was shocked to see the despair in Mum's face. In her eyes I saw raw vulnerability and a desperate plea for comfort; a look that still haunts me today. She had always been stoic in times of difficulties but it was as if this was one blow too many.

However, she found the resolve to pick up the pieces and get on with her life. By this time Kevin's twin, Georgie, who had previously left home to work in Melbourne, was now living at home with Mum and in a fragile mental state after the death of his girlfriend. His use of drugs and the death of his twin deepened his depression and increased his unpredictable behaviour. Mum tolerated his moods and tantrums. She would never have considered telling him to move out even though his presence was disruptive and negative and sometimes threatening.

In April 1984, less than six months after Kevin's death, Mum was blessed with another granddaughter when Tanya was born. My youngest brother,

Peter, by now twenty three years old, was no longer living at home and was in a relationship. One day, Peter arrived on Mum's doorstep with his baby daughter in his arms. Tanya's mother had left and Peter was unable to look after the child because he had to go out to work. Mum did not hesitate. She held out her arms for Tanya. From that day on she became Tanya's mother. She brought her up and nurtured her through her early years, effectively becoming the first mother Tanya knew.

As the years passed I suggested to Mum that she should request to have the government family allowance for Tanya paid to her instead of to the child's mother. This would have involved applying for legal custody of Tanya. Mum simply would not entertain the idea. Knowing what I know now, I can well understand why she would not do anything that was even remotely perceived as taking a mother's child from her.

Whatever costs came along in the care of Tanya she willingly paid for from her own meagre supply of money and money from Peter. She also gave her time to Tanya willingly and lovingly. With Tanya, she did the same 'grandmotherly' things she did with Sally as well as all the things a mother would do for her child. She walked Tanya to kindergarten and later to school, made sure she had the right school clothes and books, packed her lunch, helped her with school work and read her bedtime stories.

Mum was heartbroken when, several years later, she had to relinquish care of Tanya because Peter and his partner resumed their relationship. Of course, Mum was happy that Tanya was able to live with her parents again but this did not diminish the pain of separation. Apart from her natural attachment to Tanya, imagine the painful memories this must have stirred for her. Certainly, Tanya's cousin Sally recalls that her grandmother was so bereft after Peter reclaimed Tanya that she was uncharacteristically disinterested in Sally for a short time. However, Peter ensured that Mum had regular contact with Tanya. Both Sally and Tanya have treasured memories of Myrtle as a loving and caring grandmother who offered them sanctuary and comfort during childhood calamities. She brooked no nonsense and yet was not above spoiling them and could also be relied on for fun and laughter.

Chapter 21

WHILE TANYA AND SALLY WERE the grandchildren Mum was able to develop close relationships with, she did have others. My older brothers Bobby and Maxie had both married and started their families. However, there was not a lot of opportunity for contact as they both lived interstate. I can recall some of Maxie's visits with his young children. Mum made the most of her time with them: nursing them, cuddling them and playing with them. There were also the grandchildren she did not know about: the children of Bertie, Noel and Audrey. Did she wonder about them? I am sure that she did.

Bertie, after he left the technical college, became a printer with the *Queensland Times*. At the age of 26 he was a tall, handsome young man with a thick head of dark hair, twinkling eyes and a quirky sense of humour. He caught the eye of the girls, but his heart was stolen one evening at a barbecue in the 1960s when he met Lea, whom he married in 1965.

Even on his wedding day, Bertie's quirky sense of humour could not be suppressed. Standing on the church steps with his new bride he looked at the minister and said, "Right. I'm married. Now where do I go to get a divorce?" The minister did not really understand Bertie's sense of humour but, luckily, Lea did.

Bertie and Lea lived in Sydney for a short time when Bertie worked on *The Australian Newspaper*. When they returned to Brisbane in 1974, Bertie started work at Brisbane's daily *Courier-Mail*, where he stayed until he retired twenty years later. Lea and Bertie produced five grandchildren for Myrtle although she never met any of them.

Bertie, who grew up hating his mother as a result of his paternal grandmother's brain-washing, had no contact with Myrtle. It wasn't until the 1960s that he found out, through his sister, what had happened to his mother. Audrey had met one of Myrtle's Albury friends who was able to tell her the truth about what had happened. Bertie felt a deep sense of betrayal that he had been brought up to hate his mother and been told falsehoods about what had happened and about her character. Although he did not mention it, he must have also carried a heavy burden of misplaced guilt. Perhaps this was one of the things that made him resistant to the idea of getting in touch with his mother despite encouragement from Lea to do so.

Audrey, in the years that followed her meeting with Myrtle, had decided she did not want to marry. "I like my freedom too much," she wrote in one of her letters to her mother. She expressed a desire to travel and her itchy feet eventually took her to the United States of America. Audrey worked hard and saved enough money to fund her trip and, together with an Irish girlfriend, arrived in California in 1974. In San Francisco, a friendly local bus driver helped the girls find an apartment for short term lease. One evening, the two girls went to a nearby wine bar recommended by the bus driver. As soon as they walked in, Audrey saw two guys heading in their direction but she did not like the look of them so quickly devised a plan to avoid their attentions.

"Follow me," she whispered to her friend.

Audrey had spotted a young man enjoying a drink on his own at the bar. She now headed straight for him, sidled up, sat down next to him and offered him a warm smile.

"Sorry I'm late," she said to the astonished accountant from Kansas. "I'll have a glass of white wine, please."

The accountant was bemused but, nevertheless, ordered his new companion with the strange accent a glass of white wine. Audrey's girlfriend took her cue from her friend and managed to startle another young man sitting nearby who also suddenly found he had an attractive new companion with an odd accent. The two girls had a very pleasant evening with their 'dates' and left them to take a cab back to their apartment. The next morning, the astonished accountant from Kansas, whose name was Edward, knocked on Audrey's door to ask her to go out with him again that evening.

That was the start of a long and loving relation-ship. Edward and Audrey travelled all over the world together before returning to the USA in 1975 where they were married. Marriage did not stop their travelling. Edward's job took him to Saudi Arabia in 1978 where they lived for eight years. From there, they jetted off to exotic destinations every six months. Approximately a year after their arrival in Saudi Arabia, Audrey became pregnant with twins. Sadly, one twin did not survive but Edward and Audrey became the proud parents of a baby boy. Did this slow down the jetsetters? No. Even the birth of their second son, a much welcomed addition to the family in 1984, did not slow them down.

Edward and Audrey returned to America in 1986 and settled in Houston, Texas. By this time, Audrey had stopped writing to her mother thinking she had long since died. She carried with her into adulthood the feeling of shame and embarrassment at being an orphanage child. This is a sad consequence that 'care leavers commonly speak of. They felt ashamed because their parents rejected them. Many have never told the families they now live with, would never tell friends or workmates, and regard it as something to be hidden and forgotten, a shameful past that marks them as worth less than other people.' *(Orphans of the Living)*

Audrey's younger brother, Noel, remained in Ballarat apart from a short stint in Melbourne. He was restless and unsettled and was often involved in fights, being quick to take offence and quick to avenge himself. In retrospect, he describes himself as 'always looking for something but not knowing what I was looking for'.

In Ballarat he took room and board with a family that included two daughters. Through these sisters, Noel met Shirley, a vivacious blonde who took his eye and later captured his heart. He apparently 'swept her off her feet' although Shirley might dispute that claim.

It was when Noel applied for his birth certificate to fulfil the legal requirements to enable his marriage to Shirley to take place that he discovered he had a brother and a sister. However, he had no other information and did not know how to contact them or whether they were even still alive.

Noel became more settled after his marriage, particularly when he became a father in 1966. Like Bertie and Lea, Noel and Shirley produced five grandchildren for Myrtle whom she never met.

Although Noel was now secure in a strong and loving family environment, his work life was not so settled. He was forced to give up work when, while working at a local car parts manufacturer, he suffered serious injuries after being accidentally run over by a mobile crane. His body was crushed and bones were broken. He endured a long journey back to health but was no longer able to work. Once again he found himself in a fight. This time it was a court battle which he eventually won and was awarded payment for damages.

He did whatever he could to earn an income to supplement these payments; selling scrap metal, old cars and trailers. Noel was on crutches for a long time. He discovered a crutch could be very useful as a weapon much to the consternation one day of an overly persistent vacuum cleaner salesman who had apparently developed a strong attachment to Noel and Shirley's front door step.

In 1982, Noel met his siblings after Audrey tracked him down on one of her visits from Saudi

Arabia. In Noel's mind, he was meeting his sister for the first time as he had no memory of her, or his brother, from childhood. At their reunion Audrey told him about Bertie and passed on their brother's contact details.

Later, Noel contacted Bertie and drove up to Queensland to meet him. The first thing their wives noticed was the striking resemblance the brothers bore to each other. Despite not growing up together they shared the same mannerisms, their voices sounded the same and they even finished each other's sentences. Physically, they were like 'two peas in a pod' and shared a likeness with their father. The proof that they were sired by the same man was staring everyone in the face. A relative, who was around at the time that Agnes Bishop was spreading rumours that Noel was not Henry Bishop's child, saw them together and exclaimed, "How could they have got it so wrong?"

That question sums it up in relation to every aspect of what happened to Myrtle and her children and, indeed, to what happened to thousands of other children and their parents during the 'Orphanage Period' in Australia: from the 1920s to the 1990s.

Chapter 22

'WHILE GROWING UP IN THE Orphanage, I used to wish for our mother to come and take us home, where we belonged, but she never came near the place.' This comment was made by Lorraine Rodgers who was at Ballarat Orphanage. Hers was one of over 600 submissions to the Inquiry conducted by the Australian Senate in 2003 and 2004. Submissions were taken from people who, as children, had been in institutions in Australia from the 1920s to the 1990s. The 2009 report of this Inquiry, known as *Forgotten Australians*, states:

'The Committee received hundreds of graphic and disturbing accounts about the treatment and care experienced by children in out-of-home care. Like the child migrants before them, many care leavers showed immense courage in putting intensely personal life stories on the public record. Their stories outlined a litany of emotional, physical and sexual abuse, and often criminal physical and sexual assault. Their stories also told of neglect, humiliation and deprivation of food, education and healthcare. Such abuse and assault was widespread across institutions, across States and across the government, religious and other care providers.

But the overwhelming response as to treatment in care, even among those that made positive comments, was the lack of love, affection and nurturing that was never provided to young children at critical times during their emotional development.'

For many people who grew up 'in care' the Senate Inquiry offered them the chance to speak about their experiences for the first time because 'people are listening at long last'. Up until this time, many care leavers felt the rest of society were not bothered about their experiences and not interested in listening.

The experiences of those who made submissions to this Inquiry clearly show that children who grew up in institutions were not treated as individuals. There was a lack of personal interest in the child. The children were virtually anonymous. Little wonder these kids yearned for affection and 'sought caresses from strangers'.

Children in institutions grew up in an environment that taught them they were not important to anyone. The people they should have mattered most to, their parents, had apparently abandoned them. If your parents don't want you, the obvious message is: You're not worth loving, you're no good. As my sister Audrey put it, they were 'discarded' children. In *Orphans of the Living*, author Joanna Penglase states: 'When parents disappear from children's lives, the only way a child can interpret this is that the parent does not want them or care about them.'

In many orphanages children were told repeatedly by the staff that they were unwanted, no good, unlovable, stupid, wicked and even worse than that. The staff at the institutions often reinforced the message that the children were unwanted nuisances.

Mim McKey and her two sisters, all under the age of four, were placed in institutions in Melbourne, Victoria. She comments in her submission to the Inquiry: 'I was told constantly by Home staff, teachers, hosts and my mother, that I was irreparably stupid, recalcitrant, disobedient, totally unworthy of love, and always facing threats that I would be "put away" permanently.'

Lorraine Rodgers remembers the staff at Ballarat Orphanage telling her she had been put in the orphanage because her parents did not love her and 'you are not wanted by anyone'. It breaks my heart to think of children growing up believing: 'Nobody wants me. Nobody cares about me.'

Children like Audrey and Noel who grow up in institutions enter adulthood without the foundation of family and all that goes with it. They have no recorded history such as milestone memorabilia and photographs. They have no photos of themselves as babies or during their developmental stages, no school photographs, no photographs with family members. They have no family stories to prompt their memories of past events, to share and laugh about with others. They do not have any way of knowing what happened to them as children except their memories. There is no one to fill in the gaps. When we grow up in a family setting we receive reminders of our life's journey, of who we are and where we belong; reminders such as photos, siblings retelling stories, parents and grandparents retelling stories and other prompts that keep our memories strong. Institutionalised children are deprived of these precious pieces of the childhood jigsaw that most of us assume as our right.

Institutionalised children also grow up deprived of sibling relationships and parental role models. They have been robbed of the small daily intimacies that create bonds between parents and children or between siblings. They do not hear the often stated words that strengthen family connections such as: "You take after your mother." "You look just like your father did at your age." "You're so like your brother/sister/cousin." They have no one to cuddle them and reassure them during childhood illnesses. They have nowhere they can call private; nowhere to keep their 'treasures' safe. Therefore, they are unable to accumulate childhood items that they attach sentimental value to; items that might provide a link to a memory, a special occasion or a loved one.

There is no mother or father to arbitrate in childhood disputes or to make sure the older children do not take the younger children's things. Children in Homes had no control over and no say in such personal matters as how their hair was cut or what clothes they wore. Clothing was communal. Any gifts sent to the Home by the child's parents became communal property.

Frank Golding describes in his submission to the Inquiry how one day at Ballarat Orphanage 'we all queued up to get a share of a box of grapes donated by some generous person'. When he reached the head of the queue he was able to read the label on the box. It was addressed to Frank and his brothers and had been sent by their father. However, no-one had told the boys that their father had sent them this gift. In fact, until that time they had thought their father was dead. Frank did not mind sharing the grapes with the others but he was upset that he and his brothers had not been told about the gift and, more importantly, had not been told there had been communication from their father.

As with gifts from family members, personal possessions also became communal property or were either snatched by another inmate or confiscated by the staff. Even when the children managed to get locks for their bedroom lockers in the hope of stowing some treasured items away, the staff had access to the lockers and checked them whenever they wished. 'There was no way to keep precious things private. The mind was the only safe shelter that could not be invaded,' writes Frank Golding in his book, *An Orphan's Escape*.

The very intimate things that a mother or father might do for a child, such as wiping a small child's bottom after going on the potty, or giving comfort after a fall, are done if they are done at all by strangers and not necessarily by the same person each time.

Joanna Penglase writes that the children in Children's Homes lived 'loveless, desolate lives...motherless and fatherless, isolated from the community, a prey to assault and rape or simply casual and arbitrary cruelty, knowing there was no one to turn to – and knowing the sentence has years to go.'

As with those incarcerated in prisons, orphanage children were cut off from the wider society and therefore did not have the opportunity to explore and discover the world around them. They were not permitted outside the orphanage gates except for special outings. Most orphanage children went to school on the institution's grounds. Even 'going to the movies' was done within the grounds. For example, at Ballarat Orphanage a donated film projector was set up on Saturday nights. A film sent from Melbourne by rail was shown on a make-shift screen made from a white sheet pinned to the dining room wall.

Some children, especially at secondary school level, attended schools outside their orphanage grounds but even then they were cut off from the outside community. They were readily identifiable as orphanage inmates by their clothes and the staff members accompanying them. There was a stigma attached to these kids because they did not have a 'proper' family. Other children looked down on them and often jeered at them and bullied them. In most cases they were excluded from the usual social interactions within and beyond a school community.

The education that institutionalised kids received was rarely adequate. In the publication *Forgotten Australians: Supporting survivors of childhood institu-*

tional care in Australia, The Alliance for Forgotten Australians outlines the 'Denial of Educational Opportunity':

'Children in institutions generally did not receive a good, or even adequate, education. Children commonly did the domestic work involved in running the orphanage, cleaning and cooking for long hours. As well, many children were put to work earning income for the institution. Children as young as eight were often put to work on farms or in laundries run by the institution. Additionally, children who are abused or neglected, who have untreated health problems or who are subjected to constant accusations of stupidity and worthlessness find it difficult to concentrate in a learning environment.'

Children living in Homes often felt 'shame, embarrassment and secrecy' because they did not have a 'normal' family and were segregated from mainstream society. Ken Carter, who was placed in 'care' as a baby after his mother became ill, in his submission to the Senate Inquiry states: 'You just have this sense of guilt that you, as an orphan, were trash.'

Like thousands of people who grew up in orphanages, my half-siblings have not shared their deepest feelings about living in these institutions. However, the stories of those who courageously put theirs on public record by submitting to the Senate

Inquiry are so similar that we can take their stories as being representative of what happened to most children who grew up 'in care'. For example, Ray Flett's submission relates how in 1957, at the age of three, he and his four siblings were 'forcibly removed' from their parents 'by the then child welfare department in NSW' and charged with being 'under improper guardianship'.

In his submission Ray recalls: 'I had been denied all knowledge of my natural family and indeed had forgotten about the existence of my siblings, aunts, uncles, grandparents, mother and father. I had no knowledge of the history of my predecessors, who I was or where I belonged.

I became a loner and distrusted all I came into contact with. I dreamt of having a family and felt so forlorn that I just lived from day to day with no one to love or be loved by, and without purpose. At the age of seven I was abused sexually several times by at least one adolescent boy who also resided at that home.'

Ken Carter states: 'The thing that hurt me most of all was that I didn't know who I was. No one ever told me where I came from or what.'

We develop our sense of identity through our family, our culture and our community but children growing up in institutions are cut off from all these things.

Mim Mckey says, '…I despaired of ever finding any sort of personal identity, much less a "normal" place in this world.'

Children were kept under control by terror and intimidation and lived with fear on a daily basis. Consequently, many children learned to be quiet, to repress their personalities, in order to escape notice; being noticed was likely to result in physical, emotional or sexual abuse. Their sense of self was destroyed.

In his submission to the Senate Inquiry David Forbes, who was placed in a 'boys' home' at the age of eight, writes: 'We were not treated like children; we were not given any love and affection. We had no dignity. We were made to line up naked waiting for our turn in the shower – summer or winter it did not matter. We had no privacy. We were constantly threatened and made fun of. There were no celebrations – our birthdays were not even acknowledged. We had no Easter eggs – even Santa Claus abandoned us. We were not even allowed any personal possessions – not that I ever had any. We were given very little food to eat and it always tasted yuck. We were not treated like individuals and we were never called by our names.'

Childhood exuberance was curbed and controlled

by a system that was regimented and authoritarian. The children lined up together at the same time each day for activities such as meals, cleaning teeth, going to the toilet and going to bed. A child who tried to deviate from this or to use their initiative in any way was punished.

Lorraine Rodgers relates how she 'just went around like a zombie, did everything I was told to. You start to think you are no good, well that is still with me, and it will be with me until I die.'

Such conditioning moulded who the children became as adults.

'Society continually tells victims to 'get over it', or 'it's in the past'. I can assure you that the treatment of those of us who survive will not be "in the past" as long as one of us draws breath, for we suffer the consequences every second of our existence.' (Ray Flett)

Joanna Penglase wonders how different her life would have been and whether she would have become a different person and still ponders questions she will never know the answers to.

'...I feel as if there is a whole other parallel life 'out there' somewhere, the one which I didn't have with my parents, brother and sister.'

In a letter sent to Australian members of parliament in 1997, mothers who had their children taken from them wrote: 'Our children not only lost the opportunity to be loved, raised and nurtured by their own mothers, they have also suffered the loss of their family of origin, their ancestry and heritage. And their families have lost them.'

Chapter 23

IT IS EITHER A MIRACLE or testament to their resilience, determination and courage that Bertie, Audrey and Noel not only survived their childhood experiences but were able to ignore, put aside or bury the baggage they were surely burdened with. Each one of my half-siblings has led a productive life, attracted love and respect, sustained a long term marriage and established a strong family unit. Other adults who were separated from their parents as children, some of whom suffered dreadful abuse, have found life extremely difficult.

Lorraine Rodgers reported that she has been through two marriages and 'I still need counselling. I am living in fear, and that is not good for me.'

Ray Flett suffers "depression, anxiety, antisocial attitudes, and nightmares, fear of people, lack of confidence, lack of social skills and a lack of identity. I have undergone counselling for much of my adult life just so I could cope with living day to day. I cannot hold a job for long; I cannot form friendships and have been unable to complete the several educational courses I have started over the last thirty years. I am currently in such a state that I rarely leave the house for fear of my reaction to any stimuli."

Mim McKey in her submission said, 'Throughout my teenage and adult years I have been dogged with many, many illnesses. Too numerous to mention. Now the anxiety and panic attacks are increasing and I am thinking that maybe they were right and they should put me away, for I thought I was really going insane. Now I am currently undergoing counselling which is costing a small fortune, and my psychologist has assured me that there are many people institutionalised as children now seeking help, male and female…For you see, we cannot forget. I cannot forget. The nightmares won't let me.'

Maree Giles, in her submission states: 'The experience at Parramatta Girls' Home has caused me a lifetime of depression, low self-esteem, lack of confidence, the inability to trust people, and fear of authority, particularly the police and social services. But worse than any of this, my fear of living in Australia forced me to live apart from my mother. I have not lived in Australia since 1971. I lost my desire to live in my own country, because it let me down so badly.'

I wonder if Audrey, who still lives in Houston, Texas, had a sense of being let down by her country and subconsciously rejected Australia because of it.

It was Houston where I met her for the first time. In 1999, I travelled with my niece, Sally, to Texas where we met Audrey, her husband, Edward, and their two sons, Jamieson and Damien. Although Audrey, like Bertie and Noel, shares a physical resemblance to her father, I was astonished at how similar her mannerisms were to Mum's. For example, the way she moves her hands and the way she sometimes holds her head.

We met again in 2008 when Audrey, Edward and Damien visited Australia. It was shortly after this trip, in February 2009, that Audrey's much loved husband Edward passed away; only five months before the birth of his first grandchild. Edward was a gentle man who had the knack of turning strangers into friends in a matter of seconds. His passing was a painful blow not only for Audrey and her two sons but also for Sally who shared an instant rapport with her Uncle Edward.

Both of Edward's sons have now produced progeny giving Audrey three grandchildren at last count. She is enjoying her role as a grandmother immensely and relishes having two daughters-in-law whom she thinks of as her own daughters.

Ballarat is much closer to Melbourne than Houston, Texas so there have been several opportunities for me, and others in the Rowley family, to meet with Noel and his family. Shirley and Noel are also enjoying being grandparents and so far have nine grandchildren to love and spoil. Noel maintains strong, long-term connections with his 'orphanage family'. In many orphanages children did not form close friendships with the other inmates. Their living conditions were such that they lived in fear of what might happen to them next. This usually meant they were forced to put personal survival above all else. They learned to distrust others. However, Noel felt a sense of solidarity with the other children at Ballarat Orphanage. He established firm friendships which have survived to this day. Noel would dearly love to have met his mother but it was not to be.

By 1990, with her health deteriorating, Mum had cut back on her involvement with the Salvation Army. Over the next few years my sister, Irene, became her home help. Irene visited her daily, making sure she had food to eat, helping her with the household chores and with bathing. In 1995, Mum was admitted to the Orbost Hospital. She died as a result of 'respiratory failure' on April 17. Her good friend, Cathy, was still by her side at her funeral five days later as were many others who respected and loved Mum.

It was only after her death that I discovered our mother's secret. I was flabbergasted to think that Mum had a secret of any kind. Furthermore, it seemed inconceivable that this woman I knew so well, whose smile was easy on her face and whose laughter was swiftly stirred, had lived with the pain of past trauma. Yet a school friend of my two older brothers had seen, even as a child, the ghosts in her eyes. "There was always sadness behind her smile," he told me.

When I recovered from the shock of finding out that Mum had had three children before she married my father, I managed to track down her first born, Bertie, who was living on Russell Island in Queensland.

During our telephone conversation he told me that he had not thought about his mother in years but that one night recently, an image of a woman appeared before him. He thought it was his mother and when he described her to me it sounded very much like Mum. We established that the timing of the appearance of the image was very close to the time of Mum's death. Perhaps it was an imagined image and perhaps it was coincidence, but it seemed to give Bertie comfort to think his mother may have visited him after her death. It is tempting to think of

Mum as a *mrart* offering her first born one last good-bye.

Sometime after our initial phone contact, I travelled to Queensland to meet Bertie and Lea in person. I discovered that my half-brother was a handsome man with gentleness in his blue eyes and a healthy head of silver hair. Bertie was not able to give me a great deal of information about his childhood. "I don't dwell on the past," he told me. He felt unable to talk about his early life even to Lea with whom he had a strong, loving relationship. He told her he had 'locked it away'.

"I've obviously locked it away for a reason. It must be too painful," he said to her, "so it's better to leave it that way."

At three and a half years of age he would have been old enough and aware enough to feel the full impact of the trauma of being separated from his mother. Children as young as two feel an overwhelming sense of loss when their mother is taken from them whether by death or separation. Added to this profound loss was the trauma of separation from his siblings. Everything that gave young Bertie security, safety and identity had been snatched away from him. Apart from intense grief, he would also have experienced feelings of separation and abandonment, isolation, confusion and self-blame.

Throughout his childhood and probably into adulthood, he must have carried a sense of loneliness and emptiness deep within.

Bertie was seriously contemplating taking the step of contacting his mother when he received my phone call to let him know she had died. It had taken over thirty years and urging from Lea before he was ready to consider the possibility of reaching out to Myrtle and then it was too late. It is difficult for anyone who has not been in the same situation to understand the complex feelings that might have prevented Bertie from reaching out to his mother.

Perhaps we get a glimpse into Bertie's mind through Ray Flett who states: 'I had consigned many memories to the farthest recesses of my mind.' Then, without warning, at the age of twenty-nine Ray received a phone call: 'The phone call was from a person who, after an absence of 26 years, identified herself as and indeed was my natural mother. This event had a devastating effect on my life. It brought back all the memories and pain. My confidence deserted me and my life started to once again disintegrate and I had no one to turn to for help. I was torn apart by the internal conflict of whom I really was and who I had become. I tried to fit into both the world I had been educated in and the world that had been so devastatingly taken from me. I did not know who I had been most disloyal to, my adopted (sic) mother or my natural mother.'

I am sure that Bertie, who had been brought up to despise his mother and had been cared for initially by his grandparents and later by his step-mother and father, felt torn by divided loyalties.

Sadly, Bertie is no longer with us. In June 2009 he became very ill and was diagnosed with esophageal cancer. The cancer spread and attacked his liver. With his usual consideration and humility, he made Lea promise not to tell Noel and Shirley who were about to leave with their family for their annual holiday in Bali. Bertie did not want them to cancel their holiday on his account, which of course is what they would have done. On their return from Bali, Noel and his family made the trip to Queensland and were able to visit with Bertie before he passed away in September that year. He left behind his wife, Lea, and their five children who have so far produced for their parents: sixteen grandchildren, ten great grand-children and two great, great, grandchildren.

My youngest brother Peter also produced another grandchild for Mum but she died before Kade was born in 1996. Kade is a budding young fisherman in Lakes Entrance, East Gippsland where he lives with his father. His half-sister is Tanya, the granddaughter Myrtle mothered and who is now a mother herself with two boys and a girl. Her cousin Sally has thus far resisted the pull of marriage and is establishing herself as a Social Worker. Sally's mother, Irene, still lives in Orbost and also works in the health sector.

In September 1998, Kevin's twin, Georgie, was killed in a road accident, similar to the accident that killed his brother. Thankfully, this was one loss Mum did not have to endure.

Mum's first husband, Henry Bishop, died only two days after my father. He had lung cancer, apparently caused by a grain of sand getting into his lungs when he was serving in the Middle East. By the time he died on January 30, 1965, the cancer had spread to his brain. The extent to which he and his mother went to in order to exclude Audrey and Noel from his life is reflected in the death notice which lists his children but omits to mention Noel. His new wife was apparently not fully informed about her husband's first family. I suspect Audrey would not have been mentioned either had she not established contact with her father in her adult life.

Agnes Bishop's husband, John, was hospitalised in 1971 but refused to allow his wife to visit him and would not talk to her. He died the same year after surgery. Agnes Bishop suffered from dementia later in life and passed away ten years after her husband.

Mum's mother, Etti Webb, had remarried in 1939.

Her marriage to Ernest Biddell apparently did not last although I was unable to find a record of a divorce. It seems that Biddell simply made himself scarce at some point. Etti was still living in Albury when she passed away in 1970. Mum was unable to attend the funeral, possibly because of her financial situation. However, her cousin Lily wrote to her immediately after the service with a full description of the day.

For me, the unveiling of Mum's secret has been a strange, sometimes surreal, experience. For one thing I had to reposition myself in the family. I was no longer third child. I was now sixth child. At first that felt weird. Eventually, I came to the realisation that I was both third child and sixth child. That also feels a little weird but at least it is no longer confusing.

My sister Irene and I became unsure about how to respond to questions that we once answered with unswerving confidence; questions like, 'How many in your family?' As far as accepting our half-siblings, that was never an issue for us. They are Mum's children and that means they are our family and that is all there is to it. We each experienced deep regret that we had not had the opportunity to grow up with them. It is impossible to have the same sense of connection with siblings you meet for the first time as adults as those you lived with, played with, fought with, cried with and laughed with day after day, year after year.

My youngest brother's reaction was more complex than ours. In the typical fashion of an Australian country male, he does not freely share his emotions and feelings and so has not spoken about it. However, I believe Peter was initially in denial about Mum and her first three children. I think it took him some time to come to terms with the truth.

As far as I know, my two older brothers, Bobby and Maxie, are not aware of Mum's secret as they have not been in touch with the family for many years despite our efforts to find them on several occasions. Their life-journeys have taken them far away and they have not yet found the track back home.

It is only through the writing of *Mother of Ten* that I have come to realise how important it has been for Bertie, Audrey and Noel to know more about their mother and to connect with her other children. They were thrown asunder in the world. Any additional piece of knowledge about their roots and any extra family member they know about helps to anchor them and reassure them of their worth as human beings and family members. Even this small comfort would have been denied them had Mum not revealed her secret by leaving the relevant papers where my sister and I were sure to find them after her death.

I asked Mum's friend Cathy, who is now an Indigenous Pastoral Care Officer, if she had known my mother's secret but she said she had not. However, she does recall a conversation when Myrtle seemed to want to tell her something. Perhaps Mum had reached that point where, with the right prompting, she might have shared her secret. Sometimes in later years separated mothers feel able to talk about their loss.

Cheryl King, in *Releasing the Past,* states, 'I have tried for so long to bury my loss deep within myself and have not shared it with anyone until the last few years. It will always be with me. My first son will always be a part of me, just as he is a part of my other two children.'

However, Mum did not open up to her friend. Cathy regrets that at that time she did not have the skills to ask the right questions that might have opened the door for Myrtle to reveal what was buried in her heart.

Although Bertie, Audrey and Noel all bear a physical likeness to their father, I have noticed that they have each inherited qualities from their mother. In Bertie I observed the same quiet humility and gentleness that Mum had. In Audrey I see Mum's sense of fun. Noel's habit of using jokes and laughter as a shield against deeper emotions is classic Myrtle. All three have demonstrated the same lack of bitterness that I witnessed in our mother. They have all inherited Mum's strength of character and ability to move through pain and adversity to live their lives outside the shadowlands of their childhoods and beyond the ghosts that might otherwise haunt them.

Notes

Mother of Ten is a memoir in that it is a historical account written from personal knowledge. I have used my memories, the memories of others and family documents. However, I have also used imagination and supposition to fill in the gaps. Along with the stories of her first three children, I wanted to give you a glimpse of what it was like for my mother living in near isolation and poverty in the Australian bush rearing seven children while also enduring the consequences of separation from her first three children.

I have not told you about my mother because I think she was extraordinary but because she was an ordinary woman with a secret. Many ordinary women hide extraordinary secrets. I think that is especially true of women in earlier times. Sadly, what happened to Myrtle and her children was common to many women and children. It is because my mother is typical of women of her time that I think her life is worthy of study. Her story gives us all a window into the world of mothers and children who suffered the same awful loss.

I would like to think that other mothers with secrets might feel more able to share them with their families after reading Myrtle's story. Although revealing a secret can be an extremely difficult thing to do, it can be helpful. At the NSW Senate Inquiry one mother made this comment:

"I have found the inquiry to be most beneficial. A part of my life that was kept hidden for years was now being freely discussed in a public forum and the shame and stigma around my son's birth and adoption has begun to dissipate as I have been able to discuss my experiences and feelings, of which grief and rage have been the most difficult to process."

It is not only the teller of the secret who can benefit from releasing the story of lost children but also all those affected by it in any way, including the children and grandchildren and all future generations. One of the most significant and beneficial results of the publication of *Whisper My Secret* was that Bertie, Audrey and Noel learned that their mother was not the evil woman she was made out to be. Not only that but their children, Myrtle's grandchildren, now have a new version of their grandmother to hand down to future generations. Not even a million sales of the book could equal the value of that.

Real names for people who were given pseudonyms in this book are as follows:

Etti Webb: Antonia (Toni) Webb.

Henry Bishop: Keith Dopper.

Agnes Bishop: Eva Dopper.

John Bishop: Charles Dopper.

Bertie Bishop: Kenny Dopper.

Audrey Bishop: Valerie Dopper.

Noel Bishop: Allan Dopper.

Glossary

Ballarat: Ballarat has important historical significance apart from the Gold Rush because it is where the Eureka Stockade took place on December 3rd, 1854. The gold miners of Ballarat rebelled against British colonial authority, specifically the expensive and compulsory Miner's Licence. Miners, police and soldiers were killed in the battle which eventually resulted in the Miner's Licence being reduced from £8 per year to £1 per year and licensed miners were also given the right to vote. The Eureka Rebellion or Eureka Stockade is considered a key event in the development of Australian democracy and Australian identity and the principles of mateship, demonstrated by the gold diggers. The term 'digger' was later adopted by the ANZAC soldiers in World War I.

bastard file: a file used for sharpening and smoothing which has cutting teeth along a flat edge and one pointed end.

blackfella: an Australian Aborigine or Torres Strait Islander. We used this word when I was growing up as a statement of fact and sometimes with affection but not as a racist slur. However, some modern 'do-gooders' seem intent on casting this word in a negative light claiming its use to be racist against Australian Aborigines; ironic really since it is Aboriginal English.

chook house: chicken coop

care-leaver: someone who grew up in what was called 'care' (institutions such as orphanages) but who now has left that 'care'.

dunny: a colloquial term for an outside toilet. The word evolved from 'dunnekin' meaning 'dung-house' in a British dialect.

fair dinkum: (colloquial) an assertion of truth of genuineness.

Jacky: Jacky's behaviour should not be seen as a reflection on the Kurnai people. I remember them as gentle, kind people who did no harm to anyone. However, as with all communities of human beings, there are individuals who deviate from the norm. (Jacky and Lizzie are pseudonyms as I felt it would not be appropriate to use their real names.)

knacker: a person who buys old horses for slaughter.

Kurnai: (sometimes spelt Gunai or Gurnai) The Aborigines of East Gippsland belonged to the Kurnai tribe which comprised five clans.

perve: colloquial for pervert.

smoko: a colloquial word for a tea-break.

Snowy River Bandit: The Snowy River Bandit roamed the bushland along the Bonang Highway in Victoria in 1940. Armed with two rifles he held up people and stores and stole foodstuffs at Buchan, Goongerah, Tubbutt, Martin's Creek and Sardine Creek. He was arrested on 20 December 1940 and charged at Orbost before being transferred to Bairnsdale District Hospital for treatment to a self-inflicted shoulder injury.

His name was Alan Torney. After escaping from an institution in Gouldburn, NSW he had gone on the run and lived in the forests of East Gippsland surviving by shooting kangaroos, sheep and rabbits until he started his robberies. He was later certified insane and admitted to a mental hospital.

The Riverina: The Riverina is an agricultural region of south-western NSW which has been home for over 40 000 years to the Yorta Yorta people and the largest Aboriginal group in NSW: the Wiradjuri people. The district is bordered on the south by the state of Victoria and on the east by the Great Dividing Range.

The Great Dividing Range, formed 300 million years ago when Australia was still part of the ancient supercontinent of Gondwana, is one of the longest mountain ranges in the world, stretching more than 3,500 kilometres (2,175 miles). The two major rivers of the Riverina, the Murray (Australia's largest river) and the Murrumbidgee, acted as a source of food as well as a means of communication and trade for the Aboriginal people. The Yorta Yorta and Wiradjuri people fished for Murray cod and shellfish and used bark canoes for travel along the rivers.

The bark canoes gave way to paddle steamers and barges used by Europeans in the 1850s. The rivers provided a transport route linking the Riverina to markets along both rivers and to river ports in South Australia and Victoria.

Apart from the riverboats, early explorers and ancient Aboriginal cultures, bushrangers also added to the rich history of the Riverina region. Australia's infamous bushranger and folk hero, Ned Kelly, made what some consider his most daring raid in the Riverina, in February 1879. After riding overland from north east Victoria, Kelly and his gang stopped at Jerilderie and captured two local policemen. They stripped the men of their uniforms and wore the uniforms to rob the Bank of New South Wales. They then held the town captive for several days. While in

Jerilderie, Ned Kelly tried to have his 8000 word manifesto, now known as the Jerilderie letter, published. The Jerilderie letter is a condemnation of the colonial administration in Victoria and specifically the treatment of the Irish. Being unable to find the local newspaper editor, Ned Kelly left the letter with a member of the bank staff and departed, returning to Victoria with £2,000 from the bank's safe. Eighteen months later in a showdown with police at Glenrowan, Ned Kelly was shot and arrested. On November 11, 1880 he was hanged at Melbourne Gaol.

Only forty years after the hanging of Ned Kelly my mother's biological parents, Alick and Vera Mills arrived in the Riverina.

Walla Walla: an Aboriginal word meaning 'place of many rocks'. The town was established by people of German extraction. In the 1830s and 1840s large numbers of Germans left the Kingdom of Prussia for Australia to escape religious persecution and hoping for better fortunes. They formed communities in South Australia but when farmland became in short supply some families made the six week journey over 600 miles (966 kilometres) to the Riverina in covered wagons and spring carts to take advantage of land opportunities. Among them were Myrtle's grandparents, Doris and Freidrich Krautz, who made their way to Jindera in 1887, later settling in Lavington which is now part of the city of Albury. Doris was a descendant of Johann Friedrich Munchenberg who migrated from Prussia to South Australia in 1839. Etti (Toni) Webb was the first child of Freidrich and Doris.

whitefella: a non-Aboriginal person of European descent. Like the term, 'blackfella', this is an Aboriginal English term used when I was growing up without racist intent.

yakka: colloquial word for 'work'. The word evolved from 'yaga', which means work in the Yagara language (Aboriginal group in the Brisbane region).

Bibliography

Cole Christine A (editor), Kashin Jan, (illustrator), 2008, *Releasing the Past: Mothers' stories of their stolen babies*, Bondi NSW, Veljanov Printing.

Penglase J, 2005, *Orphans of the Living*, Fremantle WA, Fremantle Arts Centre Press in partnership with Curtin University of Technology.

Joanna Penglase was placed 'in care' when only eight months old. She draws on her own story as well as interviews with others and submissions to the 2004 Senate Inquiry to try to unravel how and why half a million children grew up in 'care' in twentieth-century Australia.

Jones Howard C, 2010, *Orphanage Survivors: A true story of St John's, Thurgoona*, Albury NSW

The 2004 Senate Inquiry: *Forgotten Australians: A report on Australians who experienced institutional or out-of-home care* was released in August 2004. www.aph.gov.au/Parliamentary_Business/Committ ees/Senate_Committees

Extracts from the report include:

'The Committee concluded that upwards of, and possibly more than, 500 000 Australians experienced care in an orphanage, Home or other form of out-of-home care during the last century. However, it is now considered that this figure may be an underestimate. As many of these people have had a family it is highly likely that every Australian either was, is related to, works with or knows someone who experienced childhood in an institution or out-of-home care environment.

Children were placed in care for a myriad of reasons including being orphaned; being born to a single mother; family dislocation from domestic violence, divorce or separation; family poverty and parents' inability to cope with their children often as a result of some form of crisis or hardship. Many children were made wards of the state after being charged with being uncontrollable, neglected or in moral danger, not because they had done anything wrong, but because circumstances in which they found themselves resulted in them being status offenders. Others were placed in care through private arrangements usually involving payment to the Home. Irrespective of how children were placed in care, it was not their fault.'

Recommendation 1 of the 39 recommendations:

'That the Commonwealth Government issue a formal statement acknowledging, on behalf of the nation, the hurt and distress suffered by many children in institutional care, particularly the children who were victims of abuse and assault; and apologising for the harm caused to these children.'

Recommendation 2 of the 39 recommendations:

'That all State Governments and Churches and agencies, that have not already done so, issue formal statements acknowledging their role in the administration of institutional care arrangements; and apologising for the physical, psychological and social harm caused to the children, and the hurt and distress suffered by the children at the hands of those who were in charge of them, particularly the children who were victims of abuse and assault.'

On 15 November 2009 the then Prime Minister of Australia, Kevin Rudd, issued an apology on behalf of the nation to the *Forgot-*

ten Australians and former child migrants. Mr Rudd acknowledged that 'There are tens of thousands, perhaps hundreds of thousands of these stories, each as important as the other, each with its own hurts, its own humiliations its own traumas – and each united by the experience of a childhood without love, of childhood alone.

For some, this has become a very public journey of healing. For others, it remains intensely private – not even to be discussed with closest family and friends even today.'

(State governments, churches and other agencies have also apologised to the *Forgotten Australians* and *Lost Innocents*.)

Golding Frank, *2005, An Orphan's escape*, Melbourne, Lothian Books. Frank Golding and his two brothers, all under the age of seven, were admitted to Ballarat Orphanage because of so-called 'neglect'. They spent most of their childhoods there even though their parents were alive and well and cared deeply about their children.

ABC Open; Separated: a website for Australians who have been separated from their child/children or their parents by forced adoption, to tell their stories.

Moor M, 2005, *Silent Violence: Australia's White Stolen Children*, Nathan QLD. A thesis submitted in the fulfilment of the requirement for the Doctorate of Philosophy in Arts, Media and Culture at Griffith University, Nathan, Queensland by Merryl Moor, 2005. 'This thesis contributes to feminist knowledge by testing long held and arguably patriarchal and middle class notions that white 'unmarried mothers' willingly gave away their babies for adoption in the 1950s, 1960s and early 1970s in Australia.'

Harrison, Eris Jane, 2011, *Forgotten Australians: Supporting survivors of childhood institutional care in Australia*, Alliance for Forgotten Australians.

Learn more about JB Rowley's books at:

whispermysecret.weebly.com

Other books:

JB Rowley also writes the Dusty Kent Murder Mysteries under the pen name Brigid George.

Brigid George website:

www.brigidgeorge.com

Review the Book

If you have time to post a review after you read the book, that would be enormously helpful – just a few words would be fine. Many thanks to all who have already taken the time to review my books.

About the Author

JB Rowley is an award winning writer who grew up in a small Australian town called Orbost in the state of Victoria. She spent her childhood chasing snakes and lizards down hollow logs, playing Hansel and Gretel in the bush with her brothers, climbing trees, searching the local rubbish tip for books to read and generally behaving like a feral child. To avoid her boisterous brothers she often escaped into the hayshed with a book. Stories and books played a significant part in her childhood. Favourite childhood authors included Enid Blyton, Charles Dickens and Beatrix Potter. As an adult JB has read a broad range of authors and continues to read prolifically although she now prefers audio books and ebooks.

JB still lives in the state of Victoria but is now in the capital city of Melbourne where, when she is not writing, she works as an English tutor and an oral storyteller.